GRANADA TRA`
2023-2024: A Jewel of Andalusia

The Ultimate Guide to exploring the Rich History, Culture and Top Attractions of Granada

GENEVA WALKER

Table of Contents

INTRODUCTION...6

WHY VISIT GRANADA? 10

Granada: A City of History, Culture, and Beauty *10*

HISTORY AND CULTURE OF GRANADA 14

WHEN TO GO AND HOW TO GET THERE 19

PRACTICAL FACTS AND SUGGESTIONS 25

Language and Communication.....................................*25*

Customs and Etiquette *27*

Currencies..*29*

Visa Requirements..*29*

Health and Safety Tips................................*33*

Useful Apps and Websites *35*

CHAPTER 1 42

TOP ATTRACTIONS 42

THE ALHAMBRA: THE PEARL OF GRANADA.................................43

THE CATHEDRAL AND THE ROYAL CHAPEL: THE EMBLEMS OF CHRISTIAN SPAIN 48

THE ALBAYZÍN: THE HISTORIC MOORISH QUARTER 52

THE SACROMONTE: THE GYPSY AND FLAMENCO DISTRICT 59

THE GENERALIFE: THE SUMMER PALACE AND GARDENS................66

CONCLUSION..222

INTRODUCTION

The Jewel of Andalusia had always been on my bucket list as one of my travel destinations in 2023; the magnificent city of Granada, the city of dreams and stories, where the past and the present meet in a compelling harmony. I had heard about its rich history, gorgeous architecture, lively culture, and great food. Still, I wanted to see it and experience the city based on my friend's and tourists' impressions of their visit to the fantastic city. So, I decided to take a solo journey to Granada to explore it at my leisure and find its mysteries.

Following a short flight from Madrid, I arrived in Granada on a lovely morning in July. I boarded a bus from the airport to the city center, where I had rented a charming guesthouse in the Albayzín, the historic Moorish neighborhood. As soon as I checked in, I dropped my bag and walked out to visit Alhambra, the gem of Granada.

The Alhambra is a complex of palaces and gardens erected by the Nasrid dynasty, the last Muslim rulers of Spain. It is a marvel of Islamic art and architecture, with elaborate ornamentation, lovely courtyards, and spectacular vistas. I ordered my ticket online in advance, since they sell out fast, and attended a guided tour that lasted around three hours. I was astounded by the beauty and the refinement of the Alhambra and by the myths and traditions that surrounded it. I heard about the love relationships, the intrigues, the conflicts that took place there, and the renowned individuals who lived there, such as Boabdil, the last sultan of Granada, who submitted to the Catholic Monarchs in 1492.

After viewing the Alhambra, I proceeded down to the Generalife, the summer residence and gardens of the Nasrid rulers. It was a quiet sanctuary of greenery and water, where I savored the aroma of flowers and the sound of birds. I sat on a seat and observed the view, feeling comfortable and joyful.

I resumed my stroll to the Sacromonte, the gypsy and flamenco neighborhood of Granada. It is a hillside community where many people live in cave dwellings cut into the rock. It is also famed for its flamenco performances in tiny settings called Zambra. I chose to view one of them, and I was not disappointed. It was a real and vibrant show of music and dance, with guitarists, singers, and dancers expressing their feelings with talent and elegance. I clapped along with the beat and felt shivers on my skin.

After the play, I was hungry and thirsty, so I headed to Plaza Nueva, one of the major squares of Granada. There, I spotted a tapas bar that looked pleasant and packed. Tapas are tiny foods offered with beverages in Granada, generally for free. They are a terrific opportunity to explore various flavors and ingredients of local cuisine. I ordered a glass of wine and received a dish of jamón ibérico (cured ham) as a tapa. Then I ordered another glass of wine and received a dish of tortilla de patatas (potato omelet) as a tapa. Then I ordered another glass of wine and received a dish of croquetas de bacalao (cod croquettes) as a tapa. And so forth. I savored every dish and every beverage, speaking with several kind locals who offered me advice for my following days in Granada.

I concluded my first day in Granada feeling pleased and enthusiastic. I visited some of its most famous sites, sampled its most exquisite cuisines, and met some of its most hospitable people. I had also fallen in love with its

buildings, courtyards, and fountains. You may roam about and uncover hidden jewels such as the Mirador de San Nicolás, a viewpoint that gives a breathtaking view of the Alhambra and the Sierra Nevada. You may also explore some old churches, mosques, and palaces that dot the Albaicín, such as the Church of San Salvador, the Mosque of El Bañuelo, and the Palace of Dar al-Horra.

If you wish to experience the true culture of Granada, you should not miss the Sacromonte, the gypsy quarter famed for its cave dwellings and flamenco performances. The Sacromonte is positioned on a hill facing the Alhambra, giving a unique city view. You may visit some of the caverns that have been transformed into museums, such as the Museo Cuevas del Sacromonte, where you can learn about the history and customs of the gypsy population. You may also watch a flamenco concert at one of the numerous tables (flamenco venues) that provide live performances every night. You will be amazed by the intensity and emotion of this art form that blends singing, dancing, and guitar playing.

Granada is not just a city of history and culture but also a place of beauty and environment. You can view the breathtaking landscape of the Sierra Nevada National Park, which is just a short drive from Granada. The Sierra Nevada is the tallest mountain range in mainland Spain and provides a variety of activities for all seasons. You may enjoy skiing or snowboarding in the winter, hiking or bicycling in the spring and summer, or horse riding or paragliding in any season. You may also explore some of the charming settlements that are spread across the Sierra Nevada, such as Güéjar Sierra, Monachil, or Trevélez.

Granada is also a hub of food and nightlife. You may enjoy some of the exquisite meals that are distinctive of Granada, such as habeas con jamón (broad beans with ham), tortilla del Sacromonte (omelet with refuse), remojón (salad with oranges and fish) or pinions (sweet pastries). You may also enjoy one of the finest traditions of Granada: complimentary tapas. Every time you order a drink at a bar or restaurant, you will receive a complimentary tapa (a small quantity of food) to accompany it. You may taste various tapas at different restaurants and construct your tapas trail. If you want to have some fun after supper, you may join the busy nightlife of Granada. You may discover bars, pubs, and clubs for different tastes and types in districts such as Plaza Nueva, Calle Elvira, or Pedro Antonio de Alarcón.

Granada is a city that has it all: history, culture, beauty, nature, food, and nightlife. It is a city that will amaze you with its uniqueness and charm. It is a city that will make you fall in love with it. That's why you should visit Granada.

History and Culture of Granada

Granada is a city that has seen the rise and fall of empires, the collision and fusion of cultures, and the birth and death of legends. Its rich, deep, interesting history and culture reflect its varied and colorful past.

Granada was created by the ancient Iberians, who named it Iliberis. It was taken by the Romans, who named it Illinois. The city developed during Roman administration, becoming an important commercial and administrative center. However, with the fall of the Roman Empire, Granada was attacked by different barbarian tribes, such as the Vandals, the Visigoths, and the Byzantines.

In the 8th century, Granada was taken by the Moors, who brought Islam and Arabic culture to the city. They nicknamed it Garnata al-Yahud, meaning "Granada of the Jews" because of the significant Jewish community. The Moors developed Granada into a glorious city with great palaces, mosques, gardens, and fountains. They also erected a fortification on a hill above the city called the Alcazaba.

In the 11th century, Granada became the seat of an independent Moorish country known as the Zirid dynasty. The Zirids were eventually superseded by the Almoravids and the Almohads, two great Berber dynasties who reigned over much of North Africa and Spain. In the 13th century, Granada became the final bastion of Moorish Spain, following the Christian reconquest of much of the Iberian Peninsula. The Nasrid dynasty governed the city, which reached its pinnacle under Muhammad V (1354-1391). He created the Alhambra, Granada's most renowned and magnificent palace, and other architectural wonders such as the Generalife Gardens and the Madrasa (school).

The Nasrid kingdom of Granada was an affluent and sophisticated state with a tolerant and cosmopolitan society. It was also a center of study and art, drawing intellectuals, poets, musicians, and craftspeople from all over the Islamic world. However, it was also continuously attacked by its Christian neighbors, notably Castile and Aragon. In 1469, these two kingdoms merged by the marriage of Ferdinand II and Isabella I, who became known as the Catholic Monarchs. They started a last crusade against Granada, which lasted for 10 years. In 1492, Granada succumbed to the Christian army after a protracted siege. The last Nasrid monarch, Muhammad XII (also known as Boabdil), gave the keys to the city to Ferdinand and Isabella. He subsequently went for exile in North Africa, purportedly shedding tears as he gazed back at his lost realm. This incident signaled the end of Moorish Spain and the beginning of a new era.

Granada witnessed a significant shift during Christian hegemony. The Catholic Monarchs ordered the conversion or deportation of all Muslims and Jews from the city. They also erected new churches, convents, monasteries, and mansions in Gothic, Renaissance, and Baroque styles. They also created the University of Granada in 1531, one of the oldest in Spain. One of their most notable gestures was to erect their tomb in the Royal Chapel (Capilla Real) near the Cathedral of Granada. There they were buried together with their daughter Juana (also known as Juana la Loca) and her husband Philip I (also known as Philip el Hermoso).

Granada remained an important city in Spain until the 18th century, when it faced various setbacks, such as wars, epidemics, earthquakes, and economic downfall. However, it also saw notable creative successes, such as the Granadine School of Painting, sculpture, and Architecture creation, which produced artists such as Alonso Cano, Pedro de Mena, and José de Bada y Navajas. It also inspired numerous authors, such as Washington Irving, who authored Tales of the Alhambra in 1832, a collection of tales based on his time at the palace. Another notable writer who resided in Granada was Federico García Lorca, one of the most prominent poets and playwrights of the 20th century. He was born in Fuente Vaqueros, a community near Granada, in 1898. He studied at the University of Granada and became part of the Generation of '27, a group of avant-garde artists and thinkers. He composed works such as Romancero Gitano (Gypsy Ballads), Bodas de Sangre (Blood Wedding), and La Casa de Bernarda Alba (The House of Bernarda Alba). He also supported Granada's popular culture and customs, such as the flamenco, the cante jondo (deep singing), and the fiestas. He was slain by Nationalist troops in 1936, at the beginning of the Spanish Civil War, becoming a martyr and a symbol of freedom and innovation.

Today, Granada is a sophisticated and bustling city with a population of over 230,000. It is the capital of the Granada province and one of Spain's biggest tourist sites. It draws millions of tourists annually, who come to appreciate its historical and cultural legacy, notably the Alhambra, a UNESCO World Legacy Site. Granada also provides a range of sights and activities, including museums, festivals, concerts, sports, cuisine, and nightlife. It is also a university city, with more than 80,000 students from all over the globe. Granada is a city that mixes tradition with innovation, history and culture, beauty and charm. It is a city that fascinates you and makes you fall in love.

When to go and how to get there

Granada is a city that provides something for everyone, whether you are seeking history, culture, nature, or nightlife. But when is the ideal time to visit this Andalusian gem? And how can you get there conveniently and affordably? In this chapter, we will answer these questions and help you plan your ideal vacation to Granada.

When to go

Granada has a Mediterranean climate with hot summers and moderate winters. The average temperature varies from 8°C (46°F) in January to 25°C (77°F) in July. However, owing to its position at the foot of the Sierra Nevada mountains, Granada may also suffer severe weather conditions, such as snow, frost, and heat waves.

The ideal time to visit Granada depends on your choices and interests. Here are some variables to consider:

• **Crowds:** Granada is a popular tourist destination all year round, but notably during the high seasons of Easter, summer (July-August), and Christmas. If you want to escape the crowds and enjoy a more relaxing environment, you may wish to come in the low seasons of spring (March-May) and fall (September-November). However, certain attractions may have modified opening hours or be closed during these seasons.

• **Costs:** As with other places, the costs of accommodation, transportation, and activities tend to be higher during the peak seasons and lower during the low seasons. You may also get some specials and discounts if you book in advance or go during the weekdays. If you travel on a budget, you may wish to skip the hot seasons and seek alternate choices such as hostels, flats, or campgrounds.

• **Events:** Granada offers annual festivals and events that display its rich culture and tradition. Some notable ones include the Holy Week processions in April, the International Festival of Music and Dance in June-July, the Corpus Christi fair in June, and the Día de la Cruz (Day of the Cross) in May. Book your accommodation and tickets well in advance to enjoy these events since they sell quickly.

• **Activities:** Granada provides various activities for varied tastes and seasons. If you are interested in history and architecture, you may visit the Alhambra Palace and other landmarks anytime. If you are into nature and adventure, you may explore the Sierra Nevada mountains and enjoy hiking, skiing, or cycling, depending on the season. If you seek nightlife and amusement, you may find many pubs, clubs, and restaurants in the city center and the Albaicín neighborhood.

How to get there

Granada is well-linked by many kinds of transportation. Here are some of the major options:

• **By plane:** Granada has a modest airport around 15 kilometers (9 miles) from the city center. It provides local flights to Madrid, Barcelona, Mallorca, Melilla, and Tenerife, as well as international flights to London, Manchester, Paris, Milan, Naples, Berlin, Brussels, Amsterdam, Copenhagen, Stockholm, Marrakech, Casablanca, and Istanbul. You may take a bus or a cab from the airport to the city center for roughly 3 EUR or 25 EUR respectively.

• **By rail:** Granada has a train station around 2 km (1.2 miles) from the city center. It offers high-speed trains (AVE) to Madrid (about 3 hours), Barcelona (about 6 hours), Seville (about 2 hours), Malaga (about 1 hour), Cordoba (about 1 hour), Valencia (about 4 hours), Alicante (about 4 hours), Zaragoza (about 5 hours), Murcia (about 3 hours), Almeria (about 2 hours), Jaen (about 1 hour), Linares-Baeza (about 1 hour), Antequera-Santa Ana (about 30 minutes), Loja-San Francisco (about 15 minutes), and Iznalloz (about 10 minutes). You may take a bus or a cab from the railway station to the city center for roughly 1 EUR or 10 EUR respectively.

• **By bus:** Granada has a bus terminal around 3 kilometers (1.8 miles) from the city center. It operates frequent buses to various places inside Spain and beyond. Some of the most popular ones are Madrid (about 5 hours), Barcelona (about 10 hours), Seville (about 3 hours), Malaga (about 2 hours), Cordoba (about 3 hours), Valencia (about 7 hours), Alicante (about 6 hours), Zaragoza (about 8 hours), Murcia (about 4 hours), Almeria (about 3 hours), Jaen (about 2 hours), Cadiz (about 5 hours), Algeciras (about 4 hours), Marbella (about 3 hours), Nerja (about 1 hour), Motril (about 1 hour),

Almuñecar (about 1 hour), Salobreña (about 1 hour), and Lanjarón (about 1 hour). You may also get buses to Portugal, France, Italy, Germany, Belgium, the Netherlands, Switzerland, Morocco, etc. You may take a bus or a cab from the bus terminal to the city center for roughly 1 EUR or 10 EUR respectively.

• **By automobile:** Granada is accessible through many highways and roads. The main ones are the A-92, which connects Granada with Seville, Malaga, Almeria, and Murcia; the A-44, which connects Granada with Jaen, Cordoba, and Madrid; the A-92N, which connects Granada with Guadix and Baza; the A-402, which connects Granada with Motril and Almuñecar; and the A-395, which connects Granada with the Sierra Nevada ski resort. You may locate parking places in the city center for roughly 2 EUR per hour or 20 EUR per day.

To conclude, when to travel and how to get there is an essential chapter that will help you organize your vacation to Granada. It encompasses the following aspects:

- The ideal time to visit Granada depends on your choices and interests. You may select from various seasons, rates, events, and activities.

- Granada is well-linked by several kinds of transportation. You may select from an airline, train, bus, or automobile based on your price, time, and convenience.

- Granada is a city that will amaze you with its beauty, history, and culture. We wish you a pleasant vacation and an unforgettable experience.

Practical facts and suggestions

Granada is a city of contrasts, where the old and the contemporary live harmoniously. It is a site where you can admire the towering Alhambra, meander through the small alleyways of the Albaicin, experience the bustling tapas culture, and learn the rich history and culture of Andalusia. Whether planning a short holiday or a longer stay, Granada offers something for everyone. But before you pack your bags and fly to this wonderful area, here are some practical facts and advice to help you make the most of your vacation.

Language and Communication

The official language of Granada is Spanish, although you may also hear certain Arabic words and phrases, notably in the historic Moorish neighborhood of the Albaicin. Most people in Granada speak some English, particularly in tourist areas, although it is always welcomed if you acquire some simple Spanish terms and expressions, such as:

- Hola (Hello
- Buenos días (Good morning
- Buenas tardes (Good afternoon)

- Buenas noches (Good evening/night)
- Adiós (Goodbye)
- Gracias (Thank you)
- De nada (You're welcome)
- Por favor (Please)
- Perdón/Disculpe (Excuse me/Sorry)
- ¿Habla inglés? (Do you speak English?)
- No hablo español (I don't speak Spanish)
- ¿Cómo se llama? (What is your name?)
- Me llamo... (My name is...)
- ¿Dónde está...? (Where is...?)
- ¿Cuánto cuesta? (How much does it cost?)
- ¿Qué hora es? (What time is it?)
- ¿Dónde puedo encontrar...? (Where can I find...?)
- ¿Me puede ayudar? (Can you assist me?)
- ¿Qué me recomienda? (What do you recommend?)

If you wish to study more Spanish, you may also take a language course at one of the numerous language schools in Granada, such as Don Quijote, Escuela Montalbán, or Instituto Mediterráneo Sol.

Customs and Etiquette

Granada is a pleasant and inviting city, but there are particular norms and etiquette that you should be aware of to prevent any misunderstandings or annoyance. Here are some of them:

• **Greetings:** When meeting someone for the first time, it is traditional to shake hands. If you know someone well, you may also kiss them on both cheeks, beginning with the right one. Males normally only kiss other males if they are close acquaintances or family.

• **Personal space:** Spaniards prefer to stand closer to each other than individuals from other cultures, particularly while chatting. This does not imply they are violating your personal space but rather exhibiting attention and kindness. However, you may respectfully move back or change the conversation if you feel uncomfortable.

• **Dress code:** Granada is a pretty casual city when it comes to dress code; however, there are particular times when you should dress more professionally or conservatively. For example, while visiting religious institutions such as churches or mosques, you should cover your shoulders and knees and avoid wearing shorts, skirts, or dresses that are excessively short or exposing. You should also remove your hat or sunglasses while entering these areas. When going to a fancy restaurant or a theater, you should dress carefully and avoid wearing jeans, shoes, or T-shirts.

• **Tipping:** Tipping is not necessary in Granada. However, it is appreciated if you get excellent service. The normal sum is 5% to 10% of the bill, depending on the quality of the service and the kind of business. You may leave a tip on the table or round up the total after paying. However, some businesses may add a service fee to the bill, so verify before tipping.

• **Tapas:** One of the most recognizable parts of Granada's culture is tapas, which are small amounts of cuisine served with beverages in pubs and restaurants. Tapas are frequently free in Granada as long as you purchase a drink. However, some venues may charge for or provide various tapas based on the drink you purchase. The best way to enjoy tapas is to travel from bar to bar and taste various sorts of cuisine and beverages. Tapas are frequently eaten standing at the bar or seated on stools or tiny tables.

Currencies

The currency used in Granada is the euro (€), which is split into 100 cents. There are coins of 1, 2, 5, 10, 20, 50 cents, and 1 and 2 euros. Other banknotes include 5, 10, 20, 50, 100, 200, and 500 euros. You may exchange money at banks, exchange offices, or ATMs, commonly accessible in Granada. However, you should be aware of the applicable exchange rates and costs. You may also use your credit or debit card at most businesses. However, some may charge a fee or have a minimum amount for card payments. Taking some cash with you is essential, particularly for small purchases or gratuities.

Visa Requirements

If you are a citizen of the European Union, the European Economic Area, or Switzerland, you do not require a visa to visit Granada or Spain. You merely need a valid passport or national identification card. You may remain for up to 90 days without any limitations. If you are a citizen of one of the following countries, you also do not require a visa to visit Granada or Spain for tourist or business reasons as long as your stay does not exceed 90 days within 180 days:

- Albania
- Andorra
- Antigua and Barbuda
- Argentina
- Australia
- Bahamas
- Barbados
- Bosnia and Herzegovina
- Brazil
- Brunei
- Canada
- Chile
- Colombia
- Costa Rica
- Dominica
- El Salvador
- Georgia
- Grenada
- Guatemala
- Honduras

- Hong Kong
- Israel

- Japan
- Kiribati
- Macao
- Malaysia
- Marshall Islands
- Mauritius
- Mexico
- Micronesia
- Moldova
- Monaco
- Montenegro
- New Zealand
- Nicaragua
- North Macedonia
- Palau
- Panama
- Paraguay
- Peru
- Saint Kitts and Nevis
- Saint Lucia

• Saint Vincent and the Grenadines

• Samoa

• San Marino

• Serbia

• Seychelles

• Singapore

• Solomon Islands

• South Korea

• Taiwan (with passport number beginning with 8 or 9)

• Timor-Leste -Tonga -Trinidad and Tobago -Tuvalu - Ukraine -UAE -Uruguay -US -Vanuatu -Vatican City - Venezuela

However, you will require a valid passport with at least three months of validity beyond your desired departure date from Spain. You may also need to produce evidence of adequate finances, health insurance, return or onward ticket, and housing. If you are a citizen of any other country, you must apply for a visa before coming to Granada or Spain. You may verify the prerequisites and processes on your country's Spanish Ministry of Foreign Affairs website or the Spanish Embassy or Consulate. You must give papers such as your passport, application form, picture, trip itinerary, proof of finances, health insurance, lodging, and purpose of visit. You may also need to pay a visa fee and attend an interview. The processing time may vary based on the kind of visa and the place of origin.

Health and Safety Tips

Granada is typically a safe and healthy city. However, there are certain health and safety guidelines that you should follow to prevent any complications during your visit. Here are some of them:

• **Health insurance:** If you are a citizen of the European Union, the European Economic Area, or Switzerland, you may use your European Health Insurance Card (EHIC) to access public health care services in Granada for free or at a reduced fee. However, this does not cover other medical expenditures, such as private treatment, dental care, or repatriation. Therefore, it is important to obtain supplemental travel insurance that covers these charges. If you are a citizen of any other nation, you must acquire private health insurance covering your medical requirements in Granada. You may evaluate various alternatives on websites like Allianz Care or Cigna Global.

• **Vaccines:** There are no special vaccines necessary for going to Granada. However, it is encouraged to have your usual immunizations up to date, such as tetanus, diphtheria, polio, measles, mumps, rubella, hepatitis A and B, and influenza. You may check the latest health recommendations on websites such as CDC or NHS.

• **Water:** Tap water in Granada is safe to drink, although it may have a different flavor or fragrance from what you are accustomed to. If you prefer bottled water, you may get it at supermarkets, convenience shops, or vending machines. You may also replenish your water bottle at public fountains throughout the city.

• **Food:** Food in Granada is typically healthy and tasty, but there are certain measures that you should take to prevent any food illness or allergies. For example, avoid eating raw or undercooked meat, fish, eggs, or dairy products; wash your hands before eating; peel or wash fruits and vegetables; check the expiry date of packaged goods; and advise the staff if you have any dietary requirements or allergies.

• **Sun:** Granada enjoys a sunny environment all year round; however, summer may become hot. To protect yourself against sunburns and heatstroke, use sunscreen with a high SPF rating; wear a hat and sunglasses; drink lots of water; avoid alcohol and caffeine; seek shade around noon; and wear light and loose clothes.

• **Crime:** Granada is not a hazardous city, and violent crime is infrequent. However, like in other Spanish towns, pickpocketing and petty theft are regular concerns, particularly in the big tourist districts at night. To prevent becoming a victim, you should keep a watchful eye on your belongings; use purses with zippers and sling them across your chest instead of over one shoulder; be particularly aware in crowded, touristy areas; and don't carry all of your valuables items, such as passport, money, or credit cards, in one pocket. If you are robbed or attacked, report it to the local police station or call 112.

Useful Apps and Websites

Granada is a city that provides a lot of sights and activities for tourists, but it may also take time to navigate and organize your vacation. To make your life simpler, here are some handy applications and websites that you may use to get the most out of your time in Granada:

• **Citymapper:** This app lets you identify the best route to navigate about Granada via public transit, walking, cycling, or carsharing. It offers you real-time information, maps, timetables, and pricing for numerous forms of travel. You may also evaluate various choices and bookmark your preferred routes.

• **Triposo:** This app is a travel guide that covers Granada and other places in Spain. It includes offline maps, suggestions, reviews, and advice for touring, dining, drinking, shopping, and more. You may also book excursions, activities, and tickets using the app.

• **TheFork:** This app lets you locate and reserve restaurants in Granada and other cities in Spain. You may browse by cuisine, location, price, rating, or availability. You may also receive discounts and incentives on specific restaurants and earn loyalty points for every booking.

• **Lime:** This app enables you to hire electric scooters in Granada and other cities in Spain. The app allows you to find, unlock, and pay for the scooters. It is a pleasant and eco-friendly way to tour the city.

• **Cabify:** This app is a ride-hailing service that runs in Granada and other cities in Spain. You may reserve a vehicle with a driver via the app. You may pick the kind of vehicle, view the expected price and time of arrival, then pay securely using your credit card or PayPal.

• **Bicing:** This app is a bike-sharing service that works in Granada and other cities in Spain. You can register, find, unlock, and pay for the bikes using the app. It is an affordable and healthy method to get about the city.

• **Glovo:** This app is a delivery service that works in Granada and other cities in Spain. You may order meals, groceries, beverages, or anything else that you need from local retailers and restaurants using the app. A courier will bring it to your home in minutes.

• **Too Good To Go:** This app helps you reduce food waste and save money by bringing you leftover food from local restaurants, bakeries, supermarkets, and more at discounted pricing. You may explore the available offerings near you using the app and pick up your meal at a given time.

• **Vinted:** This software lets you purchase and sell second-hand clothing online. You may explore hundreds of things from various brands and designs with the app. You may even sell your clothing by photographing and submitting them to the app.

• **Happy Cow:** This app lets you locate vegan and vegetarian eateries in Granada and other cities in Spain. You may search by location, price, rating, or kind of cuisine using the app. You may also read reviews and suggestions from other users.

Emergency Contacts In case of an emergency during your stay in Granada, here are some crucial numbers that you should know:

- Emergency: 112
- Ambulance: 061
- Fire brigade: 080
- National police: 091
- Local police: 092
- Civil Guard: 062
- Police Station: 958 80 80 00
- Fire Station: 958 80 77 77
- Coast Guard: 900 202 202
- Red Cross: 958 22 22 22
- Electricity Company: 900 333 999
- Water Company: 900 700 720
- Gas Company: 900 750 750
- Government Information Service: 958 24 83 00
- NAGICO Medical Insurance Emergency Assistance: +34 958 27 12 72
- Hospitals:
Hospital Universitario Virgen de las Nieves: +34 958 02 02 02

Hospital Universitario San Cecilio: +34 958 02 10 00

Hospital Clínico San Cecilio: +34 958 02 11 00

We hope this chapter has given you valuable information and advice for your vacation to Granada. Granada is a city that will amaze you with its beauty, charm, and variety. We are convinced you will have a wonderful time in this lovely location. Enjoy your stay!

CHAPTER 1

Top Attractions

Granada is a city that will fascinate you with its finest attractions. It offers something for everyone, whether you are interested in history, art, culture, or nature. You will be impressed by the variety and splendor of its monuments, museums, and landscapes.

Granada is a city that has seen the rise and fall of civilizations, the collision and fusion of cultures, and the birth and death of legends. The city has retained its tradition and character while embracing modernization and innovation. It is a city that provides you with a unique and memorable experience.

In this travel guide, you will discover all the information you need to explore and enjoy the finest of Granada. You will explore its finest attractions, from the towering Alhambra to the lovely Albayzín, the beautiful Cathedral to the bustling Sacromonte, and the tranquil Generalife to the adventurous Sierra Nevada.

The Alhambra: the pearl of Granada

The Alhambra is the most renowned and spectacular attraction in Granada. It is a complex of palaces and gardens that was the seat of the Nasrid monarchs, the last Muslim rulers of Spain. It is a UNESCO World Heritage Site and one of the most visited destinations in the world.

The Alhambra is perched on a mountaintop overlooking the city and the mountains. It encompasses an area of around 13 hectares (32 acres) and comprises various buildings and structures, each with its purpose and design. The primary sections of the complex are:

• **The Alcazaba:** the oldest and most defended portion of the Alhambra, which functioned as a military barracks and a watchtower. It provides magnificent views of Granada and the Sierra Nevada. You may climb to the top of the Torre de la Vela (Tower of the Candle), which was used to indicate the beginning and end of the day with a bell

• **The Nasrid Palaces:** the most magnificent and elegant component of the Alhambra, which functioned as the royal palace and court. They are separated into three sections: the

Mexuar, where administrative and judicial issues were managed; the Comares Palace, where formal banquets and ceremonies were held; and the Palace of the Lions, where private life and amusement took place. Each part has chambers, courtyards, hallways, and fountains covered with exquisite geometric designs, arabesques, calligraphy, tiles, stucco, and woodwork. Some of the more notable characteristics are:

- The Patio del Mexuar (Court of the Mexuar), with its porticoed gallery and its oratory niche facing Mecca.

- The Patio de los Arrayanes (Court of the Myrtles), with its long rectangular pool mirroring the front of the Comares Palace.

- The Sala de la Barca (Hall of the Boat), with its hardwood ceiling resembling an inverted boat hull.

- The Sala de los Embajadores (Hall of the Ambassadors), with its octagonal roof decorated with star-shaped patterns.

- The Patio de los Leones (Court of the Lions), with its renowned fountain supported by twelve marble lions.

- The Sala de los Abencerrajes (Hall of the Abencerrages), with its stalactite dome and its narrative of horrific slaughter.

- The Sala de las Dos Hermanas (Hall of the Two Sisters), with its exquisite ceiling and its mirador (viewing window) overlooking the garden.

- The Sala de los Reyes (Hall of the Kings), with its painted leather ceiling portraying hunting scenes.

• **The Palace of Charles V:** a Renaissance-style palace erected by Charles V, Holy Roman Emperor and King of Spain, in 1526. It was meant to be his house in Granada, but it was never built or occupied. It contains a circular courtyard encircled by two floors of columns. It contains two museums: the Museum of Fine Arts, which shows paintings and sculptures from the 15th to 20th centuries, and the Museum of Alhambra, which exhibits Islamic art and relics from the Alhambra and other places in Granada.

• **The Generalife:** a summer palace and gardens situated near the Alhambra. Muhammad III established it in the 14th century as a place to rest and appreciate nature. It contains multiple courtyards, pavilions, pools, fountains, flowers, and trees. Some of the highlights are:

- The Patio de la Acequia (Court of the Water Channel), with its long pool served by four jets and surrounded by flower gardens.

- The Patio de la Sultana (Court of the Sultana), with its cypress tree, where according to folklore, Boabdil's wife Zoraya met her lover.

- The Escalera del Agua (Stairway of Water) has stairs along a wall with water pipes that produce a pleasant impression.
- The Mirador Romántico (Romantic Viewpoint), with stunning views of the Alhambra and Granada.

- To visit the Alhambra, you need to book your ticket online in advance since they sell out rapidly. You may pick between several tickets based on what you want to see and when you want to go. You may also take a guided tour explaining the history and importance of each complex section. You should expect to spend at least three hours to see everything, but you may certainly spend more time if you want to appreciate it at your speed.

The Alhambra site will astound you with its beauty and refinement. It is a destination that will transfer you to another period and culture. It is a site that will make you admire the art and architecture of the Islamic world. It is a spot that you will never forget.

The Cathedral and the Royal Chapel: the emblems of Christian Spain

Granada is a city that saw a major transformation in its history, culture, and identity with the invasion by the Catholic Monarchs in 1492. The end of the Muslim rule and the foundation of the Christian monarchy signaled a new era for Granada, represented in its architecture, art, and religion. Two of the most famous landmarks that exemplify this metamorphosis are the Cathedral and the Royal Chapel, which stand next to one other in the city's center.

The Cathedral of Granada, or the Cathedral of the Incarnation, is a spectacular example of Spanish Renaissance architecture, with some Gothic and Baroque characteristics. It was commissioned by Queen Isabella I in 1505, immediately after the conquest of Granada, but its construction continued until 1704 under several architects and styles. The Cathedral is one of the biggest in Europe, with five naves, several chapels, a dome, and a tower. Its interior is notable for its vastness, light, and artwork, including paintings, sculptures, altarpieces, and stained glass windows. Some of the highlights are:

• **The Main Chapel** is behind a beautiful iron screen at the end of the central nave. It has a colossal altarpiece constructed of marble and jasper, with sculptures of saints and scenes from the life of Christ. The altarpiece was created by Diego de Siloé and completed by many painters between 1520 and 1563.

• **The Tabernacle** is a distinct structure linked to the Cathedral, where the Blessed Sacrament is housed. It features a circular layout with a dome embellished with paintings by Antonio Palomino. It also has a beautiful silver monstrance by Pedro de Mena.

• **The Chapel of Our Lady of Antigua:** It is one of the earliest chapels of the Cathedral, dating from 1523. It houses a Gothic picture of the Virgin Mary that was brought from Seville by Queen Isabella I. The image was adored by the Catholic Monarchs and their descendants as the patron saint of Granada.

The Royal Chapel, or the Capilla Real, is an Isabelline Gothic tower created between 1505 and 1517 as the burial site of the Catholic Monarchs and their successors. It was initially incorporated into the complex of the Cathedral, although it has its entrance and character. The Royal Chapel is a treasure mine of art and history, as it contains:

• **The Tombs are positioned in the church's transept**, behind marble mausoleums fashioned by Italian craftsmen. On the right side are the graves of Queen Isabella I and King Ferdinand II, and on the left are the tombs of their daughter Joanna I and her husband Philip I. Underneath are their coffins in a crypt that may be viewed.

• **The Main Altarpiece:** It is a wonderful work of art composed of alabaster, wood, and gold, with sculptures and paintings showing episodes from the lives of St. John the Baptist and St. John the Evangelist, to whom the chapel is dedicated. The altarpiece was created by Felipe Vigarny and completed by many painters between 1518 and 1521.

• **The Sacristy-Museum:** It is a chamber that retains some of the personal items and relics of the Catholic Monarchs, such as their crowns, wands, swords, books, tapestries, and paintings. Among them are several masterpieces by Flemish painters such as Rogier van der Weyden, Hans Memling, and Dirk Bouts.

The Cathedral and the Royal Chapel are two structures you should notice when visiting Granada. They are not only stunning for their aesthetic worth but also for their historical relevance. They reflect the heritage of the Catholic Monarchs, who altered the destiny of Granada and Spain forever.

The Albayzín: the historic Moorish quarter

If you want to feel the beauty and romance of Granada, there is no better spot to visit than the Albayzín, the ancient Moorish part of the city. This is where Granada's history and culture come alive amid a tangle of small lanes, whitewashed buildings, secret courtyards, and spectacular views of the Alhambra.

The Albayzín (or Albaicín) is situated on a hill opposite the Alhambra, divided by the river Darro. It was named a World Heritage Site by UNESCO in 1994, together with the Alhambra and the Generalife Gardens. The Albayzín maintains the spirit of the old Islamic city with its urban plan, architecture, and ambiance. It is also a thriving and active area where you can discover stores, cafés, restaurants, pubs, and flamenco venues.

The roots of the Albayzín extend back to the ancient Iberians, who erected the city of Iliberis on this hill. The Romans called it Illiberis, making it an important economic and administrative hub. After the collapse of the Roman Empire, the city was conquered by numerous barbarian tribes, such as the Vandals, the Visigoths, and the Byzantines.

In the 8th century, the Moors seized Granada and gave it a new name: Garnata al-Yahud, meaning "Granada of the Jews" because of the considerable Jewish community. The Moors developed Granada into a glorious city with great palaces, mosques, gardens, and fountains. They also erected a fortification on a hill above the city called the Alcazaba.

In the 11th century, Granada became the seat of an independent Moorish country known as the Zirid dynasty. The Zirids were eventually superseded by the Almoravids and the Almohads, two great Berber dynasties who reigned over much of North Africa and Spain. In the 13th century, Granada became the final bastion of Moorish Spain, following the Christian reconquest of much of the Iberian Peninsula. The Nasrid dynasty governed the city, which reached its pinnacle under Muhammad V (1354-1391). He created the Alhambra, Granada's most renowned and magnificent palace, and other architectural wonders such as the Generalife Gardens and the Madrasa (school).

The Nasrid kingdom of Granada was an affluent and sophisticated state with a tolerant and cosmopolitan society. It was also a center of study and art, drawing intellectuals, poets, musicians, and craftspeople from all over the Islamic world. However, it was also continuously attacked by its Christian neighbors, notably Castile and Aragon. In 1469, these two kingdoms merged by the marriage of Ferdinand II and Isabella I, who became known as the Catholic Monarchs.

They started a last crusade against Granada, which lasted for 10 years. In 1492, Granada succumbed to the Christian army after a protracted siege. The last Nasrid monarch, Muhammad XII (also known as Boabdil), gave the keys to the city to Ferdinand and Isabella. He subsequently went for exile in North Africa, purportedly shedding tears as he gazed back at his lost realm. This incident signaled the end of Moorish Spain and the beginning of a new era.

Granada witnessed a significant shift during Christian hegemony. The Catholic Monarchs ordered the conversion or deportation of all Muslims and Jews from the city. They also erected new churches, convents, monasteries, and mansions in Gothic, Renaissance, and Baroque styles. They also created the University of Granada in 1531, one of the oldest in Spain. One of their most notable gestures was to erect their tomb in the Royal Chapel (Capilla Real) near the Cathedral of Granada. There they were buried with their daughter Juana (also known as Juana la Loca) and her husband Philip I (also known as Philip el Hermoso).

The Albayzín was allocated to the Muslims as a place of habitation following the conquest. However, following multiple Moorish uprisings, they were ousted from Granada in 1609. Christians later repopulated the area from various regions of Spain. Many mosques were destroyed or transformed into churches. Some examples include San Nicolás (previously Alixares), San Cristóbal (formerly Almorabitin), and San Salvador (originally the Great Mosque). The affluent Christians also erected their luxurious cármenes (luxury country residences with gardens) in the Albayzín, taking advantage of the water supply and the vistas of the Alhambra.

The Albayzín remained an important and busy neighborhood until the 18th century when it experienced various setbacks like wars, diseases, earthquakes, and economic downfall. It also saw notable creative triumphs, such as the creation of the Granadine School of painting, sculpture, and architecture, which produced artists like Alonso Cano, Pedro de Mena, and José de Bada y Navajas. It also inspired numerous authors, such as Washington Irving, who authored Tales of the Alhambra in 1832, a collection of tales based on his time at the palace.

Today, Albayzín is a contemporary and bustling neighborhood with a population of over 30,000. It is one of the primary tourist attractions of Granada and provides a range of sights and activities. Here are some of the highlights that you should not miss:

The Mirador de San Nicolás: This is the most renowned viewpoint in Granada, where you can enjoy a beautiful view of the Alhambra and the Sierra Nevada mountains. It is particularly lovely at sunset when the castle walls glow crimson, and the sky is flooded with hues. You may also listen to live music provided by local musicians or attend a flamenco performance at night.

The Carrera del Darro: This is one of the most scenic avenues in Granada, following the flow of the river Darro. It is lined with historic buildings, bridges, churches, and monuments. You may stroll along it or hire a horse-drawn carriage to see its loveliness. You may also visit some of the sights along the road, such as the Bañuelo (the oldest Arab baths in Spain), the Casa de Castril (a Renaissance palace that houses the Archaeological Museum), and the Paseo de los Tristes (a lovely promenade with views of the Alhambra).

The Plaza Larga: This is the major plaza of the Albayzín, where you can find a vibrant market on Saturdays. Cafés, restaurants, stores, and pubs flank it. You may also view other noteworthy structures such as the Casa de Zafra (a 14th-century Nasrid palace that houses the Interpretation Center of the Albayzín), the Church of San Gregorio (a former mosque with a Mudejar tower), and the Arco de las Pesas (a medieval gate with a coat of arms and weights).

The Sacromonte: This is a hill near the Albayzín, where you can locate the traditional caves inhabited by gypsies. They are famed for their flamenco concerts and festivals.

You can also visit some of the attractions in this area, such as the Abbey of Sacromonte (a 17th-century monastery that contains relics of Granada's patron saints), the Museum of Sacromonte (a collection of cave houses that display the history and culture of this neighborhood), and the Cuevas del Camino del Avellano (a group of caves that offer panoramic views of Granada).

The Albayzín: the historic Moorish neighborhood (conclusion)

The Albayzín site will amaze you with its history, culture, and beauty. It is a site where you may experience the essence of Granada and uncover its secrets and treasures. It is a site where you may enjoy the greatest views of the Alhambra and listen to the sounds of flamenco. It is a location where you may enjoy the tastes of the local food and socialize with pleasant people. It is a location where you may lose yourself in the maze of streets and rediscover yourself in the enchantment of the moment.

The Albayzín is more than simply a neighborhood. It is a universe with its beauty and enchantment. It is a world that encourages you to explore it, to experience it, and to love it. It is a universe that will leave you with amazing memories and a desire to return.

The Sacromonte: the Gypsy and Flamenco district

Granada is a city that has a rich and diversified cultural past, integrating the influences of the Arab, Jewish, Christian, and Gypsy groups that have molded its history. One of the most intriguing and original areas in Granada is the Sacromonte, the home of the Gypsies and the birthplace of a distinct flamenco called Zambra.

This chapter will walk you through this colorful and distinctive region's history, customs, and attractions. We will also advise you to appreciate its vibrant environment, breathtaking vistas, and creative attitude.

Origins

The Sacromonte (literally Sacred Mountain) is situated on the slope opposite the Alhambra, overlooking the Darro River valley. It is stated that the original occupants of this neighborhood were the Moors, who were exiled from the city following the Christian conquest in 1492. They took safety in the caves created by erosion and water from the soft clay soil.

Later, in the 16th century, the Gypsies (or Gitanos) came to Granada from India and resided in the Sacromonte. They carried their nomadic lifestyle, peculiar culture, and musical prowess. They also adapted to their new surroundings by working as blacksmiths, basket makers, horse sellers, and performers.

The Gypsies lived in peace with their neighbors, the Moriscos (the converted Muslims who stayed in Spain after the Reconquista), until 1568, when a revolt broke out against the repressive policies of King Philip II. The insurrection was ruthlessly repressed, and many Moriscos were slain or banished. The Gypsies were likewise oppressed and discriminated against by the state and society.

Despite these struggles, the Gypsies kept their identity and customs in the Sacromonte. They also developed a strong sense of community and solidarity among themselves and other oppressed groups. They formed an intrinsic part of Granada's culture and history, contributing to its artistic and social variety.

Traditions

One of the most unique and recognized traditions of the Sacromonte is flamenco. Flamenco is a sophisticated and passionate art style incorporating singing, dancing, guitar playing, and clapping. It evolved in Andalusia due to synthesizing numerous musical elements, such as Arabic, Jewish, Christian, and Gypsy.

The Gypsies of the Sacromonte created their kind of flamenco, called Zambra. Zambra means "party" or "celebration" in Arabic, and it refers to a joyous gathering when music and dancing are performed. Zambra is defined by its rawness, emotion, and spontaneity. The dancers are barefoot and use hand castanets instead of shoes to denote the beat. The vocalists improvise songs that represent their feelings and experiences. The guitarists accompany them with complicated melodies and chords.

Zambra was originally performed in private houses or caves at important events, such as weddings, baptisms, or religious festivals. However, during the 20th century, zambra has also become a major tourist destination. Many caverns have been turned into tables (flamenco venues) where professional artists conduct nightly entertainment for guests. Some of the most notable tablaos in the Sacromonte are Venta el Gallo, Cuevas los Tarantos, Cuevas la Rocío, and María la Canastera.

Another notable ritual of the Sacromonte is Semana Santa (Holy Week). This religious event remembers the passion, death, and resurrection of Jesus Christ. It takes place during the week before Easter and comprises processions of floats bearing sculptures of saints or scenes from the Bible. The processions are accompanied by bands playing sad music and penitents wearing hoods and carrying candles or crosses.

The most prominent procession of the Sacromonte is that of Cristo de los Gitanos (Christ of the Gypsies). It takes place on Holy Wednesday night and involves a statue of Jesus bearing his crucifixion. The statue is carried by Gypsy men dressed in black who walk barefoot over a carpet of rosemary. The procession proceeds through the small lanes of the Sacromonte amid shouts, prayers, and flamenco melodies. The climax of the procession is when it reaches an open spot called El Llano de la Cruz (The Plain of the Cross), where a bonfire is lit and fireworks are released.

Attractions

The Sacromonte provides several attractions for travelers who wish to learn about its history, culture, and environment. Here are some of the important ones:

The Abbey of Sacromonte: This is a 17th-century monastery that was erected on top of an old catacomb where some remains of Saint Cecilio (the patron saint of Granada) and other martyrs were recovered. The abbey features a church, a museum, and a library that hold priceless artworks and manuscripts. It also gives panoramic views of the city and the mountains.

The Museum of Sacromonte: This museum highlights the history and lifestyle of the Gypsies of the Sacromonte. It comprises many caverns that have been refurbished and equipped with traditional artifacts and instruments. It also showcases exhibitions on flamenco, crafts, religion, and culture.

The Caves of Sacromonte: These traditional residences of the Gypsies dug into the mountainside. They feature a modest, pleasant interior with whitewashed walls, wooden beams, and fireplaces. Families still inhabit some, while others are available to tourists or hired as lodging. Staying in a cave is a unique and genuine way to discover the Sacromonte.

The Nature of Sacromonte: The Sacromonte is surrounded by a wonderful natural setting that inspires exploration and relaxation. It has several hiking trails that lead to scenic spots, such as the Mirador de San Miguel Alto (a viewpoint that offers stunning views of the Alhambra and the city), the Fuente del Avellano (a spring where poets and artists used to gather), and the Barranco de los Negros (a gorge where Gypsies used to hide during the persecution). It also features a river beach where you may swim or sunbathe.

To conclude, the Sacromonte: the Gypsy and flamenco area is a chapter that will show you one of the most intriguing and original districts in Granada. It encompasses the following aspects:

- Sacromonte was founded by the Moors and the Gypsies who lived there after being exiled or persecuted by the Christian authority.
- The traditions of the Sacromonte, notably flamenco and zambra, are distinctive and expressive art forms that mix singing, dancing, guitar playing, and clapping. You will also learn about Semana Santa, the religious event incorporating floats and sculpture processions.

- The attractions of the Sacromonte, such as the Abbey of Sacromonte, the Museum of Sacromonte, the Caves of Sacromonte, and the Nature of Sacromonte. You will explore the history, culture, and lifestyle of the Gypsies, as well as experience the breathtaking vistas and environment of the region.

The Generalife: the summer palace and gardens

The Generalife is one of the most attractive spots in Granada, a city that is rich in treasures. The Nasrid sultans' summer residence and country estate reigned over the last Muslim kingdom in Spain until 1492. The name Generalife means "the architect's garden" in Arabic, but its exact origin is still a mystery. What is known is that this site was built as a paradise on earth, where the sultans might enjoy the beauty of nature, the freshness of the water, and the tranquillity of seclusion.

The Generalife is built on the slope opposite the Alhambra, the major palace complex of the Nasrids. It is linked to the Alhambra by a covered walkway that traverses the gorge of the Darro River. The Generalife consists of two primary parts: the palace and the gardens. The palace is a small tower that has been changed and rebuilt.

It contains two courtyards: the Patio de la Acequia (the Water Garden Courtyard) and the Patio de la Sultana (the Sultana's Courtyard). The Water Garden Courtyard is Generalife's most renowned and spectacular feature. It contains a large pool that runs down the center axis of the courtyard, bordered by fountains, flower gardens, and pavilions. The river reflects the sky and the surrounding structures, creating a calm and tranquil mood. The Sultana's Courtyard is smaller and more personal. It contains a circular pool surrounded by cypress trees and flowers. According to folklore, here was where one of the sultans' wives had an affair with a knight of the Abencerrajes family, who were rivals of the Nasrids.

The gardens of the Generalife are a masterwork of landscape design. They mix aspects of Islamic, Renaissance, and Romantic styles, representing the numerous historical eras and influences that formed Granada. The gardens are separated into numerous parts, each with character and beauty. Some of the more significant portions are:

The Lower or New Gardens: These gardens were established in 1931 to replace an area that required restoration. They feature cypresses, myrtles, roses, vines, and stones placed in geometric designs. They also include four ponds in the form of a cross that depict the four rivers of heaven in Islamic mythology.

The Spanish-Muslim Garden: This garden is an homage to the original style of the Nasrids, who employed plants and water as aesthetic features. It features fruit trees, flowers, herbs, and vegetables that give color, aroma, and nourishment. It also features a small pond with water lilies and fish.

The Dismounting Yard: This is the entrance to the Generalife from the Alhambra. It features two courtyards: one with vines and flowers and another with orange trees and a fountain. It also includes a black, green, blue, and white door with a magnificent mosaic.

The Cypress Courtyard: This courtyard is situated behind the palace and includes a big cypress tree over 600 years old. It is reported that this tree saw the love affair between the sultana and the knight.

The Water Staircase: This staircase links lower and higher gardens. It features water channels flowing along its barriers, producing a refreshing and harmonious effect. It also contains arches and niches embellished with tiles and plasterwork.

The Romantic Mirador: This mirador or vista is situated at the highest point of the Generalife. It gives a panoramic view of Granada, including the Alhambra, the Albayzin, and the Sierra Nevada mountains. It was erected in 1836 by an English architect influenced by Romanticism.

The Generalife is a spot that beckons you to rest, reflect, and dream. It is a location where you can experience the history and culture of Granada on every corner. It is a spot that will fascinate you with its beauty and charm.

CHAPTER 2

Museums and Art Galleries

Granada is a city that will inspire you with its museums and art galleries. It has a rich and diversified creative past, from the Islamic art of the Alhambra to the modern art of the Centro José Guerrero. You will discover works of art that represent Granada's history, culture, and identity, as well as works of art that question, provoke, and innovate.

Granada is a city that has been a crossroads of civilizations, a melting pot of cultures, and a birthplace of creativity. It has been affected by the Iberians, the Romans, the Visigoths, the Arabs, the Jews, the Christians, and many others. It has been home to artists such as Ibn Zamrak, Alonso Cano, Manuel de Falla, Federico García Lorca, José Guerrero, and many more. It has been a source of inspiration for artists such as Washington Irving, Henri Matisse, Pablo Picasso, and many more.

In this travel guide, you will discover all the information you need to visit and enjoy Granada's top museums and art galleries. You will discover about their collections, their exhibits, their opening hours, and their costs. You can also discover advice and suggestions on how to make the most of your stay.

The Museum of Fine Arts: the oldest in Spain

Granada is a city that has a rich and diversified creative legacy due to its long and stormy past. From the Moorish beauty of the Alhambra to the Renaissance splendor of the Cathedral, Granada delivers a feast for the eyes and the spirit. But if you want to find the hidden treasures of Granada's art, you should visit the Museum of Fine Arts, the oldest public museum in Spain.

The Museum of Fine Arts of Granada was formed in 1839 following the takeover of the estates and artworks of the religious orders by the liberal administration of Mendizábal. The museum was first situated in the old convent of Santa Cruz la Real. Still, it relocated numerous times until it settled in its present location: the second floor of the Palace of Charles V, near the Alhambra, in 1958.

The museum includes nearly 2,000 works from the 15th to the 20th century. Most works are paintings and sculptures, but there are also examples of other methods, such as tapestry, engraving, and ceramics. The museum is organized into nine rooms, organized chronologically and thematically. Some of the highlights are:

Room I shows pieces from the late 15th and early 16th centuries inspired by Flemish art. It comprises a magnificent polychrome wood ensemble showing the Lamentation over Christ, credited to Jacobo Florentino.

Room II is devoted to Alonso Cano, the most important artist of Granada in the 17th century. He was a painter, sculptor, and architect, and his works demonstrate his command of light, color, and arrangement. Some of his masterpieces include The Immaculate Conception, The Crucifixion, and Saint John of God.

Room III: It shows works by followers and contemporaries of Alonso Cano, such as Pedro de Mena, Juan de Sevilla, and José de Mora. They perpetuated the heritage of religious painting in Granada, specifically focusing on realism and emotion. A great example is The Ecstasy of Saint Teresa by Pedro de Mena.

Room IV includes works from the 18th century, marked by a more secular and ornamental style. It features landscapes, portraits, and still lifes by painters such as Antonio

Palomino, Mariano Salvador Maella, and Miguel Jerónimo de Cieza.

Room V comprises works from the 19th century inspired by Romanticism and Realism. It displays works by local painters such as Mariano Fortuny, José María López Mezquita, and José María Rodríguez-Acosta.

Room VI: It displays paintings from the late 19th and early 20th centuries inspired by Granada's landscapes and landmarks. It comprises works by foreign painters who visited or resided in Granada, such as John Frederick Lewis, Henri Regnault, and Gustave Doré.

Room VIII: It showcases works from the first half of the 20th century, highlighted by avant-garde movements such as Cubism, Surrealism, and Expressionism. It features works by painters such as Manuel Ángeles Ortiz, Ismael González de la Serna, and José Guerrero.

Room IX: It features works from the second half of the 20th century and beyond, representing current movements such as Abstract Expressionism, Pop Art, and Conceptual

Art. It features works by painters such as Manuel Rivera, Antonio López García, and Juan Vida.

The Museum of Fine Arts is a must-see for everyone who likes art and wants to understand more about Granada's cultural past. It is not just a museum that maintains and shows important artworks but also a museum that tells a narrative: the tale of Granada's history, culture, and identity.

The Science Park: an interactive and educational museum

If you are searching for a fun and instructive way to spend a day in Granada, you can take advantage of the Science Park. This interactive and educational museum will excite both children and adults. The Scientific Park is the first interactive scientific museum in Andalusia and one of the most visited in Spain. It occupies more than 70,000 square meters and provides a range of displays, activities, and attractions relating to many science disciplines, such as physics, chemistry, biology, astronomy, and ecology.

The Science Park was opened in 1995 and has been developing ever since. Its director is Ernesto Páramo Sureda, who is also the originator of the idea for the development of the park and its subsequent additions. The park boasts contemporary and inventive architecture, with many structures linked by green spaces and pathways. The park also contains a planetarium, an observation tower, a butterfly house, a biodome, and a tropical forest.

The major attraction of the Science Park is its interactive displays, meant to immerse visitors and inspire educational enjoyment. You may touch, explore, play, and learn with more than 300 displays covering mechanics, electricity, magnetism, optics, sound, light, heat, energy, matter, life, health, perception, communication, environment, and culture. You may also enjoy live demonstrations and seminars that explain scientific phenomena in an accessible and enjoyable manner.

Some of the highlights of the Science Park are:

The Foucault's Pendulum Building: This is the primary entry to the park, where you can witness a Foucault pendulum that depicts the earth's rotation. You may also explore the development of the cosmos from the Big Bang to the current day and uncover some of our world's ecosystems.

The Explore Building: This is where you can find most of the interactive displays that address different elements of science. You may also view some temporary exhibits that vary throughout the year.

The Perception Hall: This is where you may test your senses and challenge your intellect with optical illusions, riddles, games, and experiments. You may also learn about how our brain operates and how it influences our behavior.

The Human Body Hall: This is where you may learn about the structure and function of our body and its organs. You may also view some of the developments in medicine and biotechnology that enhance our health and quality of life.

The Eureka Hall: This is where you may have fun with physics and mathematics. You may play with mechanical games, electric circuits, magnetic fields, and geometric forms. You may also view some of the innovations and discoveries that have transformed the history of science and technology.

The Biosphere Hall: This is where you may learn about the variety and complexity of life on earth. You may view some living organisms that occupy diverse ecosystems, such as the ocean, the forest, the desert, and the polar areas. You may also learn about the issues and hazards threatening our world and its ecosystems.

The Planetarium is where you can watch a stunning presentation that recreates the sky and the stars. You may also learn about astronomy and space exploration. The Planetarium features a dome with a diameter of 10 meters and a capacity for 80 people.

The Observation Tower is where you can enjoy a panoramic view of Granada and its surroundings. You may also witness some natural atmospheric phenomena, such as clouds, rainbows, lightning, and eclipses. The tower has a height of 50 meters and a capacity for 20 passengers.

The Butterfly House: This is where you may view more than 150 species of butterflies from all over the globe. You may also observe some of the plants and flowers that attract them. The butterfly house has a surface area of 2,000 square meters and a temperature of 25 degrees Celsius.

The Biodome: This is where you may witness more than 200 types of animals and plants from various locations on the earth. You may also learn about biodiversity and conservation. The biodome comprises four zones that imitate diverse environments: coral reefs, mangroves, tropical forests, and Madagascar. The biodome has a surface area of 4,000 square meters and a capacity of 300 persons.

The Tropical Forest: This is where you may experience the temperature and flora of a tropical jungle. You may also observe some of the species that reside there, such as toucans, sloths, lemurs, crocodiles, and frogs. The tropical forest has a surface area of 1,500 square meters and a temperature of 28 degrees Celsius.

The Science Park: an interactive and informative museum (conclusion)

The Science Park is a destination that will excite you with its interactive and informative displays. It is a place where you may explore the marvels of science and learn about the world and yourself. It is a location where you may have fun with your family and friends and have a wonderful day in Granada.

The Federico García Lorca House Museum: the birthplace of the great poet

Granada is a city that has inspired many artists and authors throughout history, but none more so than Federico García Lorca, one of the most famous and renowned poets and playwrights of the 20th century. Lorca was born in Granada in 1898 and spent his infancy and adolescence in the region, where he formed his literary sensibility and his affection for the culture and customs of Andalusia.

Suppose you wish to understand more about Lorca's life and writings. In that case, you should visit the Federico García Lorca House Museum in the hamlet of Fuente Vaqueros, some 17 kilometers (10.5 miles) from Granada. This is the home where Lorca was born on June 5, 1898, and lived his early years until his family relocated to Granada in 1909.

The home museum was established in 1986 during the centennial of Lorca's birth. It has been repaired and furnished with genuine artifacts and furnishings that belonged to the poet and his family. It also showcases images, papers, manuscripts, sketches, paintings, and personal artifacts that reflect Lorca's history and creative career.

The home museum consists of two stories and a courtyard. On the ground level, you can see the living room, the dining room, the kitchen, and the pantry. On the first level, you can view the bedrooms, including Lorca's room, where he penned some of his early poetry. The patio is a traditional Andalusian courtyard featuring a well, a fountain, and a garden.

The home museum also conducts cultural events such as exhibits, concerts, seminars, talks, and guided tours. It also holds an annual poetry contest for young authors. The home museum is part of a network of cultural sites devoted to Lorca in Granada, together with the Huerta de San Vicente, where he spent his summers; the Federico García Lorca Centre, where his manuscripts are conserved; and the Federico García Lorca Park, where he is interred.

In conclusion, the Federico García Lorca House Museum: the birthplace of the renowned poet, is a chapter that will take you to the house where Lorca was born and where he lived in his early years. It encompasses the following aspects:

- The history and importance of the home museum, how it was launched in 1986, and how it has been refurbished and equipped with genuine antiques and furniture that belonged to the poet and his family.

- The contents and characteristics of the home museum, including pictures, papers, manuscripts, sketches, paintings, and personal artifacts, reflect Lorca's history and creative career. You will also view the living room, the dining room, the kitchen, the pantry, the bedrooms, and the terrace.

- The cultural activities and events that the house museum conducts, such as exhibits, concerts, seminars, talks, and guided tours. You will also learn about the yearly poetry contest for young authors and the network of cultural organizations devoted to Lorca in Granada.

The Caja Granada Cultural Center: a contemporary and versatile location

If you seek a contemporary and multipurpose place that provides a broad choice of cultural and educational programs, you should visit the Caja Granada Cultural Center. This facility is part of the Caja Granada Foundation, a social and cultural organization that supports the growth and well-being of the people of Granada and Andalusia.

The Caja Granada Cultural Center is set in a beautiful tower created by the famous architect Alberto Campo Baeza, who also designed the nearby Museum of Memory of Andalusia. The structure is a big horizontal box of concrete with a 42-meter-high screen that functions as a façade and a landmark. The facility contains many amenities that appeal to diverse interests and requirements, such as:

The CajaGranada Theater: This theater is a cultural reference in Granada, presenting numerous events like movies, concerts, drama, children's theater, conferences, and more. The theater has a capacity of 400 seats and is equipped with state-of-the-art equipment and sound systems. Check the monthly schedule of events on the website1 or at the box office.

The Temporary Exhibition Hall: This hall displays temporary exhibits of diverse creative genres, such as painting, sculpture, photography, video art, and more. The exhibits are mainly connected to the Museum of Memory of Andalusia topics, such as history, culture, identity, and diversity. You may also discover information about the current and forthcoming exhibits on the website1 or at the reception.

The Plaza of Cultures: This plaza is an open-air place that supports diverse creative manifestations, such as concerts, dance performances, poetry readings, and more. The plaza is surrounded by water canals and flora, providing a nice and soothing ambiance. You may enjoy the activities for free or for a symbolic charge.

The Workshop Rooms: These rooms are intended for holding workshops, courses, seminars, and other educational events for persons of all ages. The rooms have tables, seats, projectors, computers, and other items. You may find information about the various workshops on the website1 at the reception.

The oval Patio: This patio is positioned in the middle of the structure and has an oval form that evokes the Palace of Charles V patio in the Alhambra. The terrace is utilized for holding events such as book presentations, award ceremonies, press conferences, and more. It also acts as a gathering spot and a resting space for guests.

The Caja Granada Cultural Center is a venue that allows you to investigate, study, enjoy, and participate in the cultural life of Granada. It is a site representing the variety and depth of Andalusia's history and character. It is a destination that will impress you with its unique architecture and its extensive schedule of activities.

The Alhambra Museum: a collection of Islamic art and artifacts

The Alhambra Museum is situated on the ground level of the Palace of Charles V, near the Alhambra ticket office. It is a museum that displays Islamic art and relics from Alhambra and other locations in Granada. It is a museum that will show you the artistic and cultural legacy of the Nasrid dynasty, the last Muslim ruler of Spain.

The museum comprises seven rooms, grouped in historical sequence from the 11th to the 16th centuries. Each room contains a selection of pieces that illustrate the different aspects of Islamic art and society, such as religion, politics, economy, science, and daily life. Some of the artworks are original, while others are replicas or reconstructions. Some sculptures are placed in displays, while others are embedded into the walls or the floor. Explanation panels accompany some works, while others are left to your imagination.

The museum features a collection of nearly 1,500 artifacts, including pottery, textiles, metals, woodwork, coins, weaponry, and jewelry. Some of the more notable compositions are:

- The marble capital from the Almoravid era (11th-12th centuries) is adorned with botanical themes and Arabic inscriptions.

- The bronze astrolabe from the Almohad era (12th-13th centuries) was utilized for astronomical and astrological calculations.

- The ceramic vase from the Nasrid period (13th-15th centuries), with a blue and white geometric pattern and a poem extolling its beauty.

- The silk brocade from the Nasrid era (13th-15th centuries), with a crimson and gold flower design and an inscription with the motto of the Nasrid kings: "There is no victor but God."

- The hardwood ceiling from the Nasrid era (13th-15th centuries), with a star-shaped dome and a carved lattice.

- The ivory pyxis from the Nasrid era (13th-15th centuries), with a cylindrical form and a cover with a knob. It was used to hold fragrances or cosmetics.
- The marble fountain from the Nasrid era (13th-15th centuries), with a basin supported by eight columns and a spout in the form of a lion's head.

- The ceramic tile from the Nasrid period (13th-15th centuries), with a green and yellow geometric pattern and an inscription with the name of Muhammad V, one of the most significant Nasrid monarchs.

- The metal candlestick from the Nasrid era (13th-15th centuries), with a hexagonal base and a stem with rings and knobs.

- The wooden chest from the Mudejar era (15th-16th centuries), with a rectangular form and a cover with hinges. It was used to hold papers or valuables.

Please book your ticket online to visit the Alhambra Museum since they sell out rapidly. You may pick between several tickets based on what you want to see and when you want to go. You may also take a guided tour to explain each artwork's history and importance. You should expect to spend at least one hour seeing everything, but you may certainly spend more time if you want to appreciate everything quickly.

The Alhambra Museum is a destination that will wow you with its beauty and uniqueness. It is a location that will tell you about the Islamic art and culture that influenced Granada. It is a site that will enhance your visit to the Alhambra complex. It is a spot that you will enjoy.

CHAPTER 3

Food and Drink

Granada is a city that will thrill your palette with its cuisine and beverages. Granada's cuisine reflects its history, culture and location, blending influences from the Moorish, Jewish and Christian traditions and the adjacent regions of Andalusia, Murcia and Castile. Granada's cuisine is also inspired by its climate and surroundings, employing fresh and seasonal foods from the lush plains of the Vega, the Sierra Nevada mountains and the Mediterranean shore.

In this chapter, you will discover the diversity and complexity of Granada's food, from its renowned tapas to its characteristic meals, from its local wines to its unusual spices. You will also learn about the history and origins of some of the most famous dishes, as well as some advice and suggestions on where and how to eat them.

Whether you are searching for a traditional or a contemporary experience, a savory or a sweet delight, a light or a heavy supper, Granada offers something for you. Granada is a city that will fulfill your hunger with its cuisine and beverages. It is a city that will amaze you with its variety and excellence. This city will make you want to come back for more.

What to eat in Granada: traditional foods and Specialties

Granada is a city that will please you with its cuisine. It boasts a rich and diverse cuisine inspired by its history, terrain, and culture. You will discover recipes that mix the tastes of the sea and the mountains, the scents of the fruits and the spices, and the traditions of the Muslims, the Jews, and the Christians.

In this travel guide, you will discover everything you need to eat properly in Granada. You will learn about its distinctive foods and specialties, ingredients and preparation, history and significance. You will also discover suggestions and recommendations on where to consume them, from the greatest restaurants and tapas bars to the most genuine markets and stores.

Here are some of the delicacies and specialties that you should not miss in Granada: Habas with Jamón: This is one of the most characteristic meals of Granada, prepared with fava beans cooked with onion, garlic, bay leaf, paprika, olive oil, salt, and pepper, and topped with slices of cured ham. It is a simple yet tasty recipe that displays the excellence of local goods. The beans are soft and creamy, while the ham lends a salty and smokey flavor. You may eat it as a main meal or as a tapa.

Plato Alpujarreño: This is a substantial cuisine from the Alpujarras mountains, suitable for chilly days or after a trek or ski. It consists of potatoes cooked with onion, green pepper, garlic, olive oil, salt, and pepper (patatas a lo pobre), followed by fried eggs, cured ham (jamón serrano), blood sausage (morcilla), sweet pepper (pimiento rojo), and chorizo. It is a substantial and delightful meal that offers energy and comfort. You may find it at numerous restaurants and pubs in Granada.

Tortilla del Sacromonte: This is a particular omelet from the Sacromonte district, where many gypsies dwell in cave homes. It comprises mutton brains (sesos de Cordero), nuts (Nueces), and occasionally ham (jamón) or chorizo. It is a meal that has historically been provided by the gypsies to people who trek up the Sacromonte hill on Saint Caecilius's day (January 22) to commemorate their patron saint. This meal needs an experimental taste but is worth trying for its unusual flavor and texture. You may eat it at several of the Zambra (flamenco venues) in Sacromonte.

Remojón Granaíno: This delightful salad marries the tastes of the sea and the fruits. It consists of cooked fish (bacalao), onion (cebolla), olives (aceitunas), hard-boiled egg (huevo duro), orange slices (naranja), and pomegranate seeds (Granada). It is seasoned with olive oil (aceite de oliva), vinegar (vinagre), salt (sal), and occasionally garlic (ajo). It is a cuisine that stems from the Muslim culture since they brought oranges and pomegranates to Spain. It is also popular in other provinces of Andalusia, such as Málaga, Almería, and Jaén. You may eat it as an appetizer or as a light dinner.

Olla de San Antón: This is a stew created from pork leftovers from the annual pig slaughter at the beginning of each year. It comprises pork ribs (costillas de cerdo), pig tail (rabo de cerdo), pork ear (oreja de cerdo), pork skin (piel de cerdo), black pudding (morcilla), white beans (alubias blancas), rice (arroz), mint (hierbabuena), salt (sal), and water (agua). It is cooked patiently until everything is soft and tasty. It is a meal on January 17 to mark Saint

Anthony's Day (San Antón), although you can also get it in select places throughout winter.

These are some of the meals and delicacies you may eat in Granada, but there are many more you can discover as you explore and see Granada. Granada is a city that will satisfy your hunger and your curiosity. It is a city that will give you a range of tastes and ingredients, from the traditional to the creative, from the local to the worldwide. It is a city that you will appreciate.

Where to dine in Granada: the top restaurants and tapas bars

Granada is a city that will entice you with its history, culture, and beauty. But it will also lure you with its food, which reflects its broad and colorful history. Granada is famed for its tapas, the tiny appetizers that accompany every drink and that are typically served for free. But it also provides a range of other foods inspired by the Moorish, Jewish, Christian, and Gypsy traditions that have molded its character. Whether you are seeking a quick nibble, a full dinner, or a gourmet dining experience, Granada offers something for every taste and budget. Here are some of the top places to dine in Granada in 2023-2024:

Restaurante Más Que Vinos: This wonderful tiny bar/restaurant is around the corner from the major streets and worth visiting. Their wine selection is good and moderately priced, and their tapas are crafted utilizing top ingredients. You may taste some of their specialties, such as the croquettes, the cheese board, the cod fritters, or the meatballs. They also feature a daily menu that varies according to the season and the market. The service is courteous and responsive, and the ambiance is warm and relaxing. A nice spot to have some excellent cuisine and wine in Granada

- Address: Calle Tundidores, 10, 18001 Granada
- Phone number: +34 958 56 09 86 Website: Restaurante Mas que Vinos

Bodegas Castañeda: This is a typical tapas establishment packed with locals. Spanish tile, dark wood, a bull's head on the ceiling, and portraits of matadors establish the tone in this classic tapas tavern. Enjoy a big supper in a setting with a terrific vibe. You may get some of their renowned montaditos (little sandwiches), such as the solomillo al whiskey (pork loin with whisky sauce) or the pringá (a combination of pig flesh and fat). You may also sample some of their cold cuts, cheeses, salads, or fried foods. Don't forget to wash it all down with some of their homemade vermouth or wine. A must-visit for tapas lovers in Granada

- Address: Travesia Almireceros 1-3, Esquina Plaza Sillería, Granada, 18010
- Phone number: +34 958 21 54 64 Website: Bodegas Castañeda

Taberna La Tana: This is a hidden treasure in Granada, where you can get some of the greatest wines in town. The proprietor is a sommelier who will walk you through his wide and well-chosen wine collection. You may select from various locations, kinds, and styles of wine and combine them with some of their excellent tapas. You may also order any of their cheese or ham platters or some of their handmade meals, such as the lentil stew or the meatballs. The space is tiny and pleasant, with wooden barrels and wine bottles covering the walls—a fantastic spot to explore new wines and tastes in Granada.

- Address: Calle Virgen del Rosario 11 Bajo, Esquina Placeta del Agua, Granada, 18009
- Phone number: +34 958 22 52 48 Website: Taberna La Tana

Bar Los Diamantes: This is one of the most popular tapas places in Granada, particularly among seafood lovers. They provide big amounts of fresh fried fish and shellfish, such as squid, anchovies, shrimp, clams, mussels, or octopus. You may order some of their salads, omelets, or meat meals. The location is often full and boisterous, but it adds to the fun and real feel. You have to be fast and pushy to grab a table or a space at the bar, but it is worth the effort—a terrific spot to have some of the greatest seafood in Granada.

- Address: Calle Navas 28, 18009 Granada
- Phone number: +34 958 22 70 70 Website: Bar Los Diamantes

Where to dine in Granada: the top restaurants and tapas bars (conclusion)

Granada is a city that will satisfy your hunger with its tasty variety of food. It is a city where you may experience the tradition of tapas, the tiny meals that accompany every drink and that are typically served for free. It is also a city where you can taste the impact of the Moorish, Jewish, Christian, and Gypsy cultures that have molded its identity. Whether you are seeking a quick nibble, a full dinner, or a gourmet dining experience, Granada offers something for every taste and budget.

What to drink in Granada: local wines and beers

Granada is a city that understands how to enjoy life, and one of the greatest ways to do so is by enjoying its native wines and beers. Whether you are searching for a refreshing drink to complement your tapas, a refined wine to match your dinner, or a craft brew to enjoy the local tastes, Granada offers something for you.

In this chapter, we will introduce you to some of the most popular and traditional beverages in Granada and some of the finest venues to taste them. We will also offer some ideas on how to drink like a local and make the most of your trip.

Wines

Granada has a long and rich wine-making culture that stretches back to the Roman era. The province of Granada features four wine regions: Contraviesa-Alpujarra, Montes de Granada, Vino de Calidad de Granada, and Vino de la Tierra Norte de Granada. Each area has unique traits and varietals, producing wines ranging from dry whites to luscious reds.

Some of the most prevalent grape varietals in Granada are:

Vijiriega: A white grape that yields fresh and fruity wines with floral and citrus characteristics. It is predominantly cultivated in the Contraviesa-Alpujarra area, benefiting from the high altitude and the Mediterranean environment.

Tempranillo: A red grape that creates full-bodied and complex wines with red fruit, spice, and leather aromas. It is commonly farmed throughout Spain, particularly in Montes de Granada, where it mixes nicely with other local grapes like Garnacha or Cabernet Sauvignon.

Moscatel: A white grape that yields sweet and fragrant wines with honey, apricot, and orange flower aromas. It is predominantly cultivated in the Vino de Calidad de Granada area, used to produce dessert wines or liqueurs.

Romé: A red grape that yields light, delicate wines with cherry, raspberry, and violet aromas. It is a native grape of Granada and is mostly cultivated in the Vino de la Tierra

Norte de Granada area, where it exhibits its terroir and identity.

Some of the greatest venues to experience Granada's wines are:

Bodegas Castañeda: A traditional tavern that provides a broad range of wines by the glass or bottle and exquisite tapas and cured meats. It is situated in the middle of the city, near the Cathedral.

La Tana: A tiny wine bar specializing in organic and natural wines from Granada and other parts of Spain. It also provides handmade tapas and cheese platters. It is situated in the Realejo neighborhood.

Los Diamantes: A popular tapas bar that provides substantial quantities of fried fish, shellfish, meat, and a drink of wine or beer. It has multiple sites in the city core.

La Oliva: A contemporary restaurant that provides a unique and seasonal cuisine based on local goods and a tailored wine selection showcasing Granada's wines. It is situated in the Albaicín neighborhood.

Beers

Granada is also a city that loves beer, particularly when it comes with a complimentary tapa. The most frequent beer in Granada is Alhambra, a lager made in the city since 1925. Alhambra offers numerous kinds, such as Alhambra Especial (a golden beer with a balanced taste), Alhambra Reserva 1925 (a premium beer with a powerful character), or Alhambra Sin (a non-alcoholic beer).

However, in recent years, Granada has also experienced the growth of the craft beer sector, with many microbreweries making their brews using local ingredients and innovative formulas. Some of the most renowned craft beers in Granada are:

Puchero: A craft brewery that manufactures beers using natural and organic components, such as barley, wheat, hops, yeast, water, honey, fruits, spices, or herbs. Some of their beers include Puchero Rubia (a blonde ale with citrus overtones), Puchero Tostada (a brown ale with caramel notes), or Puchero Negra (a stout with coffee notes).

Nazari: A craft brewery that crafts beers influenced by the history and culture of Granada, notably by its Arab background. Some of their brews include Nazari IPA (an Indian pale ale with flowery and fruity scents), Nazari Trigo (a wheat beer with banana and clove tastes), or Nazari Albaicín (a spiced beer with cinnamon and cardamom overtones).

Cervezas 69: A craft brewery that manufactures beers with a fun and provocative approach, employing memorable names and labels. Some of their beers include Cervezas 69 Rubia (a blonde ale with a smooth taste), Cervezas 69 Morena (a brown ale with a roasted flavor), or Cervezas 69 Picante (a chili beer with a spicy kick).

Some of the greatest venues to drink Granada's beers are:

La Taberna de Kafka: A literary-themed tavern that provides a range of beers, both local and foreign, as well as literature, board games, and live music. It is situated on the Plaza de la Romanilla, near the Cathedral.

La Botillería: A contemporary and fashionable bar that provides a large range of beers, wines, cocktails, and tapas, as well as a patio with views of the Alhambra. It is situated in the Plaza Nueva.

La Cervecería de Colón: A classic and spacious pub that serves a vast range of beers on tap or by the bottle, as well as typical tapas and raciones. It is situated in the Plaza de Colón.

El Bar de Fede: A pleasant and welcoming bar that provides a range of artisan beers, wines, and spirits, as well as vegan and vegetarian tapas and entrees. It is situated in the Realejo neighborhood.

To end this sub chapter, what to Drink in Granada: local wines and Beers is a chapter that will take you to some of the most popular and characteristic beverages in Granada and some of the finest venues to experience them. It encompasses the following aspects:

- The wines of Granada how are created in four separate areas with varied characteristics and varietals, such as Vijiriega, Tempranillo, Moscatel, and Romé.

- The beers of Granada how to encompass both the classic Alhambra lager and the rising craft beers from local microbreweries, like Puchero, Nazari, and Cervezas 69.

- The places to drink in Granada, how they provide a range of atmospheres, vistas, and tapas to complement your beverages, such as Bodegas Castañeda, La Tana, Los Diamantes, La Oliva, La Taberna de Kafka, La Botillería, La Cervecería de Colón, and El Bar de Fede.

Where to drink in Granada: the greatest bars and clubs

Granada is a city that knows how to have fun, particularly when drinking and partying. Whether searching for a comfortable pub, a fashionable cocktail bar, or a vibrant nightclub, you will find many alternatives to fit your mood and taste. Here are some of the greatest places to drink in Granada, grouped by location and category, along with their addresses and phone numbers:

Plaza Nueva and Calle Elvira: This location is one of Granada's most popular and important areas for drinking and socializing. It draws a mixed audience of residents and visitors who appreciate the variety of taverns, pubs, and tapas eateries that line the streets. Some of the greatest places to drink in this neighborhood are:

Bar Batan: This bar is a staple in Granada, providing a comfortable and welcoming ambiance, a broad range of beers and spirits, and live music every night. You may play pool, darts, or board games with your buddies. Pub Batan is situated on Calle Pedro Antonio de Alarcon 55, and you may phone them at 680 39 58 99.

Hanalei Cocktail Bar: This cocktail bar is a hidden treasure in Granada, giving a tropical and exotic ambiance, a unique and tasty selection of drinks, and fantastic service. You may also enjoy live music, DJ performances, or karaoke nights. Hanalei Cocktail Bar is situated on Calle Molinos 20, and you may phone them at 958 22 55 65.

La Qarmita - Bookshop, Coffee & Events: This facility is a mix of a bookshop, a coffee shop, and a cultural center, giving a warm and intellectual ambiance, a range of books and periodicals, and excellent coffee and tea. You may also attend activities such as book presentations, poetry readings, or seminars. La Qarmita is situated on Calle Águila 20, and you may phone them at 958 27 12 72.

Pedro Antonio de Alarcón: This street is the core of the student nightlife in Granada, providing inexpensive beverages, energetic music, and a joyful and casual feel. If you want to party hard and meet new people, it is the best location. Some of the greatest places to drink on this street are:

CAFE bar La Rocka: This bar is one of the most popular among students, featuring a rock and metal motif, a wide screen for sporting events, and a patio for smokers. You may also enjoy live music or DJ performances on weekends. CAFE PUB La Rocka is situated on Calle Pedro Antonio de Alarcon 70, and you can phone them at 640 37 36 70.

Paripé: This pub is popular with students, featuring a contemporary and colorful design, a choice of beverages and cocktails, and a dance floor with commercial hits or electronic music. You might also discover specials on beverages or free admittance on select evenings. Paripé is situated on Calle Pedro Antonio de Alarcon 31, and you may phone them at 958 25 05 25.

Efecto Club: This club is one of the greatest locations to dance in Granada, featuring a big facility with two floors, a VIP room, and a patio. You may enjoy various styles of music depending on the night, such as techno, house, reggaeton, or pop. Efecto Club is situated on Calle Pedro Antonio de Alarcon 59, and you can phone them at 958 25 05 25.

Albaicín This district is the oldest and most picturesque in Granada, affording breathtaking views of the Alhambra and the city. It is also home to some of the greatest pubs and clubs in Granada, where you can experience the traditional atmosphere of Andalusia. Some of the greatest places to drink in this area are:

La Hermosa: This brewery tap restaurant is one of the greatest venues to experience local craft beers in Granada, featuring 10 taps with diverse tastes and flavors. You may also eat classic foods like Spanish paella or croquettes. La Hermosa is situated on Plaza Aliatar 4, and you may phone them at 958 22 55 65.

Eshavira Club: This club is one of the greatest venues to listen to live music in Granada, presenting jazz, blues, flamenco, rock, or funk events every night. You may also enjoy beverages at affordable pricing and nice service. Eshavira Club is situated on Calle Postigo de la Cuna 2, and you may phone them at 958 29 08 29.

La Tertulia: This bar is one of the most iconic in Granada, giving a bohemian and cultural ambiance, a range of wines and beers, and events such as theatrical performances or art exhibits. You may also enjoy live music ranging from folk to rap. La Tertulia is situated on Calle Pintor López Mezquita 3, and you may phone them at 958 29 08 29.

Whether searching for a comfortable pub, a contemporary cocktail bar, or a vibrant nightclub, you will find many alternatives to fit your mood and taste in Granada. Granada is a city that knows how to have fun, particularly when drinking and partying. We hope you enjoy your stay in this magnificent city and enjoy exploring its nightlife possibilities. Cheers!

CHAPTER 4

Shopping and Entertainment

Granada is a city that will fascinate you with its shopping and leisure alternatives. It boasts a wide choice of stores, marketplaces, theaters, cinemas, and other venues where you may find what you are searching for, whether a souvenir, a present, a play, or a party. You will have fun and enjoy the ambiance of Granada, day and night.

The city offers something for every tourist and traveler, regardless of your taste, budget, or mood. You may shop for local handicrafts, such as pottery, leather, wood, or silver, or for worldwide names, such as Zara, Mango, or H&M. You may see a movie or a play in Spanish or English, or listen to live music or comedy performance at one of the numerous pubs and clubs. You may dance to diverse music types, from flamenco to rock, from salsa to techno, or relax with a drink and a talk with your friends.

In this travel guide, you will discover all the information you need to shop and have fun in Granada. You will learn about the finest locations and regions to purchase souvenirs and handicrafts, clothing and accessories, books and music, and more. You will also learn about the finest locations and venues to see a movie or a play, listen to live music or comedy performances, dance or drink with friends, and more.

What to purchase in Granada: souvenirs and handicrafts

Granada is a city that will fascinate you with its beauty, its history and its culture. But it is also a city that will lure you with its shopping choices, particularly if you seek souvenirs and handicrafts representing Granada's distinct culture and tradition. In this chapter, you will discover what to purchase in Granada, where to get it and how to barter. You will also learn about the history and significance of some of the most usual items and some suggestions and ideas on how to pick them. Whether searching for a souvenir for yourself or a present for someone else, Granada offers something for you.

- One of the most recognizable mementos of Granada is the terrace, a method of inlaying wood with bits of ivory, bone, metal or other materials, producing geometric or floral designs. The terrace is a relic of Moorish art and artistry, which reached its height at the Alhambra. You may buy terrace objects like boxes, trays, tables, chessboards and mirrors at numerous stores and booths across the city, notably in the Alcaicería, the ancient silk market close to the Cathedral. The costs vary according to the object's size, quality and design, but you can anticipate spending between 10 to 100 euros for a terrace item. You should search for the mark "Artesanía de Granada" (Craftsmanship of Granada), ensuring the product's authenticity and quality.

- Another popular souvenir of Granada is the pottery, inspired by the Moorish design and hues. The ceramics are constructed with clay and glazed with varying colors of blue, green, yellow and white, generating geometric or floral designs. You may buy ceramic goods like plates, bowls, cups, vases, tiles and fountains in various stores and workshops across the city, notably in the Albaicín, the historic Moorish neighborhood. The costs vary according to the piece's size, quality and design, but you can anticipate spending between 5 to 50 euros for a ceramics item. You should search for the mark "Artesanía de Granada" (Craftsmanship of Granada), ensuring the product's authenticity and quality.

- A third distinctive remembrance of Granada is the leather items, similarly influenced by the Moorish history and craft. The leather items are created using high-quality leather that is tanned, colored and embossed with diverse designs and themes. You may purchase leather items like purses, wallets, belts, coats and shoes in various stores and marketplaces across the city, notably in Plaza Bib-Rambla, Plaza Nueva and Plaza Larga. The costs vary based on the object's style, quality and design, but you may anticipate spending between 10 to 100 euros for a leather item. You should search for the mark "Artesanía de Granada" (Craftsmanship of Granada), ensuring the product's authenticity and quality.

Other souvenirs and handicrafts that you may purchase in Granada are:

- **Silverware:** Granada has a rich legacy of silverwork, reaching back to the Roman era. You may buy silver objects like jewelry, silverware, trays and decorations in various stores and workshops across the city, notably in Plaza Nueva and Calle Zacatín. The costs vary based on the thing's weight, quality and design, but you can anticipate spending between

20 to 200 euros for a silver item. You should check for the hallmark "925", which shows that the object is made of sterling silver.

- **Textiles:** Granada has a strong textile legacy inspired by the silk manufacture that thrived during the Moorish era. You may purchase textile goods like scarves, shawls, carpets and tapestries in various stores and booths across the city, notably in Plaza Bib-Rambla and Calle Elvira. The costs vary based on the product's material, quality and design, but you can anticipate spending between 10 to 100 euros for a textile item. You should search for natural fabrics such as silk, wool or cotton.

- **Spices:** Granada has a spicy cuisine that includes a range of spices such as cumin, saffron, paprika and cinnamon. You may get spices at various stores and marketplaces across the city, notably in Plaza Larga and Calle Calderería Nueva. The costs vary based on the product's kind, quality and amount, but you can anticipate spending between 1 to 10 euros for a spice item. You should choose fresh and fragrant spices stored in sealed bags or containers.

- **Sweets:** Granada has a sweet craving that stretches back to the Moorish and Jewish confectionery traditions. You may get sweets like marzipan, nougat, candied fruits and pastries in various stores and bakeries across the city, notably in Plaza Bib-Rambla and Calle Reyes Católicos. The costs vary according to the kind, quality and amount of the goods, but you may anticipate spending between 5 to 20 euros for a sweet item. You should opt for homemade and natural sweets wrapped in paper or boxes.

When you purchase souvenirs and handicrafts in Granada, you should bear in mind certain guidelines and recommendations:

- **Bargaining:** Bargaining is frequent in Granada, particularly at marketplaces and booths. You may attempt to negotiate the price of the goods with the vendor, but you should do so quietly and respectfully. You should also have a realistic estimate of the worth of the product and be prepared to walk away if you don't reach an agreement.

- **Quality:** Quality is crucial when purchasing souvenirs and handicrafts in Granada. You should seek things built with superior materials, artistry and design. You should also search for labels, trademarks or certifications that certify the authenticity and quality of the goods.

- **Variety:** Variety is another thing you should consider when purchasing souvenirs and handicrafts in Granada. You should search for distinctive, original and expressive things of Granada's culture and identity. You can also seek things that fit your taste, style and budget.

Granada is a city that will inspire you with its souvenirs and handicrafts. It is a city that will give you a vast selection of things representing its history, culture and art. It is a city that will make you want to take a piece of it home.

Where to buy in Granada: the best markets and stores

Granada is a city that fascinates you with its history, culture, and beauty. But it will also thrill you with its shopping choices, which are as broad and colorful as its history. Granada provides a range of marketplaces and stores where you may discover anything from traditional crafts and souvenirs to current fashion and design. Whether you are searching for a bargain, a present, or a treat for yourself, Granada offers something for every taste and budget. Here are some of the top locations to shop in Granada in 2023-2024:

The Alcaicería: This is the historic silk market of Granada, going back to the Moorish period. It is near the Cathedral, amid a network of little streets and lanes. It was previously a vast market where merchants from all over the globe sold silk, spices, money, and gems. However, following a fire in 1843, it was reduced to a smaller area and rebuilt in a neo-Moorish style. Today, it is one of the most famous tourist sites in Granada, where you can discover a variety of stores offering handicrafts, pottery, leather items, jewelry, lamps, carpets, and souvenirs. You may also observe the architecture and décor of the market, with its arches, tiles, and fountains—an excellent site to enjoy the ambiance and beauty of the old Granada.

- Address: Calle Alcaicería 1-3, 18001 Granada
- Phone number: +34 958 22 49 12 Website: [The Alcaicería]

The Albaicín: This is the historic Moorish neighborhood of Granada, perched on a hill opposite the Alhambra. It was named a World Heritage Site by UNESCO in 1994, together with the Alhambra and the Generalife Gardens. The Albaicín maintains the core of the ancient Islamic city, with its urban plan, architecture, and ambiance. It is also a thriving and active area where you can discover stores, cafés, restaurants, pubs, and flamenco venues. The Albaicín is an excellent spot to browse for antiques, art, literature, apparel, accessories, and ethnic items. You may also discover some of the greatest views of the Alhambra from its viewpoints (miradors), such as San Nicolás or San Cristóbal—a fantastic site to learn the history and culture of Granada.

- Address: Plaza Larga s/n, 18010 Granada
- Phone number: +34 958 22 52 48

The Plaza Bib-Rambla is one of Granada's principal squares, situated in the heart of the city center. It was previously the location of the main entrance of the Moorish city and the scene of various public events, including bullfights, tournaments, and executions. Today, it is a bustling and scenic plaza surrounded by cafés, restaurants, stores, and flower booths. You can also see some monuments and buildings that adorn the square, such as the Fountain of the Giants, the Cathedral, and the Royal Chapel. The Plaza Bib-Rambla is a great place to shop for flowers, chocolates, pastries, and ice cream. You can also enjoy local specialties, such as the pinions (small cakes soaked in syrup) or the churros con chocolate (fried dough sticks with hot chocolate)—a great place to relax and enjoy the atmosphere and flavor of Granada.

- Address: Plaza Bib-Rambla s/n, 18001 Granada
- Phone number: +34 958 22 49 12

The Calle Recogidas: This is one of the major shopping avenues in Granada, where you can discover a range of businesses, from local boutiques to worldwide names. You can shop for clothes, shoes, accessories, cosmetics, books, electronics, and more. You may also locate some department shops and shopping malls in Granada, such as El Corte Inglés, Zara, H&M, and Fnac. The Calle Recogidas is a bustling and vibrant street where you can experience the noise and bustle of the city. You may also stop and have a coffee or a snack at one of the numerous cafés and bars along the road. An excellent spot to buy anything you need in Granada.

- Address: Calle Recogidas s/n, 18002 Granada
- Phone number: +34 958 22 49 12

The Mercado de San Agustín is the oldest and biggest market in Granada, where you can discover a vast choice of fresh and local items. You may purchase fruits, vegetables, meat, fish, cheese, bread, spices, and more. You may also enjoy some of the distinctive foods of Granada, such as the tortilla de sacrament (omelet with brains and offal), the habeas with jamón (wide beans with ham), or the puchero (stew with chickpeas and beef). The Mercado de San Agustín is a vibrant and bustling location where you can mix with the inhabitants and experience the fragrances and sensations of Granada. You may also visit some of the sites nearby, such as the Corral del Carbón (a 14th-century caravanserai), the Madraza (a former Islamic school), or the Plaza Nueva (the oldest Plaza in Granada).

- Address: Plaza de San Agustín s/n, 18001 Granada
- Phone number: +34 958 22 49 12

The Alhambra store: This is the official store of the Alhambra and Generalife complex, where you can purchase various souvenirs and items associated with this wonderful landmark. You may purchase books, guides, maps, posters, postcards, calendars, magnets, keychains, mugs, t-shirts, caps, scarves, jewelry, pottery, lamps, carpets, and more. You may also locate some copies of the antiques and artworks featured in the Alhambra Museum. The Alhambra Shop is a location where you can purchase excellent things that represent the beauty and history of Alhambra. You may also assist with its protection and promotion by purchasing from this store.

- Address: Calle Real de la Alhambra s/n, 18009 Granada
- Phone number: +34 958 22 79 34

The Calle Elvira is one of the oldest and most picturesque alleys in Granada, where you can discover a blend of cultures and customs. It was formerly the principal thoroughfare of the Moorish city and, afterward, the Jewish district. Today, it is a bustling and cosmopolitan street where you can find stores, cafés, restaurants, bars, and tea houses. The Calle Elvira is an excellent spot to buy handicrafts, spices, tea, perfume, jewelry, and apparel. You may also discover some of the unique items of Granada, such as the terrace (wooden inlay work), the fajalauza (ceramic ceramics), or the zoo (leather goods). You may also enjoy music and entertainment filling the street, such as flamenco, jazz, or rock. An excellent site to explore the richness and liveliness of Granada.

The Mercado de Artesanía: This is a modest yet attractive market every Sunday morning in Plaza Nueva. The Association of Artisans of Granada organizes it and shows some of the greatest handcrafted items in the city.

You may discover a range of objects, such as paintings, sculptures, pottery, leather goods, jewelry, textiles, and more. You may also meet some craftspeople who produce them and learn about their skills and inspiration. The Mercado de Artesanía is a location where you can discover unique and unusual goods representing Granada's art and culture.

The Calle Mesones: This is one of the busiest and most commercial avenues in Granada, where you can discover various businesses, from local boutiques to worldwide names. You may shop for clothing, shoes, accessories, cosmetics, books, gadgets, and more. You may also locate some department shops and shopping malls in Granada, such as El Corte Inglés, Zara, H&M, and Fnac. The Calle Mesones is a contemporary and vibrant street where you can experience the hustle and bustle of the city. You may also stop and have a coffee or a snack at one of the numerous cafés and bars along the road. An excellent spot to buy anything you need in Granada.

- Address: Calle Mesones s/n, 18001 Granada
- Phone number: +34 958 22 49 12

Where to shop in Granada: the greatest markets and stores, with locations and phone numbers of where to shop (conclusion)

Granada is a city that will amaze you with its shopping choices, which are as rich and colorful as its history. Granada provides a range of marketplaces and stores where you may discover anything from traditional crafts and souvenirs to current fashion and design. Whether you are searching for a bargain, a present, or a treat for yourself, Granada offers something for every taste and budget.

What to do in Granada: festivals & events

Granada is a city that celebrates its culture, history, and identity through festivals and events throughout the year. Whether interested in music, dancing, art, religion, or cuisine, you will find something to fit your taste and mood in Granada. In this chapter, we will introduce you to some of the most popular and characteristic festivals and events in Granada and some of the finest spots to enjoy them. We will also offer suggestions for participating and having fun like a native.

Festivals

Granada has a rich and diversified festival schedule that represents its ethnic background and its creative culture. Some of the most prominent festivals in Granada are:

The International Festival of Music and Dance: This is one of Spain's oldest and most prominent cultural events, going back to 1883. It takes place every year in June and July, and it offers performances by famous artists from numerous genres and disciplines, such as classical music, flamenco, ballet, opera, jazz, world music, and contemporary dance. The festival also provides free performances and events in many places across the city, such as the Alhambra castle, the Generalife grounds, the Cathedral, the Royal Chapel, the Plaza de las Pasiegas, or the Plaza Bib-Rambla.

The Corpus Christi Fair is one of the most prominent religious and social festivities in Granada, going back to the 16th century. It takes place every year in June, coinciding with the feast of Corpus Christi (the Body of Christ). It comprises a week-long festival with processions, bullfights, pyrotechnics, music, dances, rides, games, vendors, and cuisine. The fair is hosted at the Recinto Ferial (the fairground) near the bus station. The fair's centerpiece is the Tarasca (a dragon-like creature that holds a mannequin dressed in the newest fashion) that marches through the city center on Wednesday morning.

The Día de la Cruz (Day of the Cross): This classic and beautiful event occurs every year on May 3. It consists of adorning crosses with flowers, fruits, ceramics, and other things and exhibiting them in public areas such as streets, squares, balconies, or patios. The crosses are assessed by a jury and awarded for their uniqueness and beauty. The event also incorporates music, dancing, costumes, and food. Some of the greatest spots to observe the crosses are the Plaza del Carmen (the City Hall Square), the Plaza Bib-Rambla (the Flower Market Square), and the Albaicín area.

The Fiesta de San Cecilio (Feast of Saint Cecilio): This festivity commemorates Saint Cecilio (the patron saint of Granada) every year on February 1. It consists of a trip to the Abbey of Sacromonte (where his remains are stored) followed by a liturgy and a benediction. The festival also incorporates music, dancing, bonfires, fireworks, and food. The characteristic cuisine of this occasion is olla de San Antón (a stew prepared with beans, pork, rice, and sausages).

Events

Granada also offers several events throughout the year, demonstrating creativity and variety. Some of the most important events in Granada are:

The Zaidín Rock Festival: This is one of Spain's oldest and most popular rock events, going back to 1980. It takes place every year in September in the Zaidín neighborhood (one of the most alternative and cosmopolitan neighborhoods in Granada). It comprises performances by local and national bands from diverse genres such as rock, pop, punk, metal, indie, or hip hop. The event also provides free entrance and camping amenities.

The Jazz Festival: This is one of Europe's most prominent jazz events, going back to 1980. It takes place every year in November at different venues across the city, such as the Teatro Isabel la Católica (the Isabel la Católica Theater), the Centro Cultural Manuel de Falla (the Manuel de Falla Cultural Center), or the Plaza de las Pasiegas (the Pasiegas Square). It comprises performances by renowned jazz stalwarts and young stars from diverse genres such as swing, blues, fusion, or avant-garde.

The Poetry Festival: This is one of Spain's most prominent poetry festivals, going back to 2004. It takes place every year in May at several venues throughout the city, such as the Huerta de San Vicente (the summer residence of Federico García Lorca), the Centro Federico García Lorca (the Federico García Lorca Center), or the Palacio de los Condes de Gabia (the Palace of the Counts of

Gabia). It comprises readings, recitals, seminars, talks, and concerts by poets from other nations and languages and homage to Granada's poets like Federico García Lorca, Luis Rosales, or Elena Martín Vivaldi.

The Tapas Route: This gourmet event takes every year in March at different taverns and restaurants across the city. It presents a specific tapa (a small dish) and a drink for a predetermined price. The tapas are reviewed by a jury and awarded for their quality and uniqueness. The event also incorporates music, entertainment, and awards for the participants. The greatest spots to enjoy the tapas route include the Realejo district, the Plaza Nueva, and the Calle Navas.

To end this sub chapter, things to Do in Granada: festivals and Events is a chapter that will show you some of the most popular and characteristic festivities in Granada and some of the finest venues to enjoy them. It encompasses the following aspects:

The festivals of Granada how represent its multicultural background and creative cultures, such as the International

Festival of Music and Dance, the Corpus Christi Fair, the Día de la Cruz, and the Fiesta de San Cecilio.

The events of Granada how to display its originality and variety, such as the Zaidín Rock Festival, the Jazz Festival, the Poetry Festival, and the Tapas Route.

Where to have fun in Granada: theaters and movies

Granada is a city that provides a lot of fun and amusement for tourists, particularly when it comes to theaters and movies. Whether searching for a cultural presentation, a comedy performance, or a blockbuster movie, you will discover many alternatives to fit your interests and budget. Here are some of the top locations to have fun in Granada, grouped by category and location, along with their addresses and phone numbers:

Theaters Granada has a great theatrical legacy, going back to the 16th century when the first theater was established in the city. Today, Granada has multiple theaters that hold diverse acts, including plays, musicals, operas, ballets, and more. Some of the top theaters in Granada are:

Teatro Isabel la Católica: This theater is one of the oldest and most famous in Granada, situated near Plaza Nueva in the city's center. It has a capacity of 650 seats and a classical design. It features national and international shows of diverse genres, such as theater, comedy, musicals, flamenco, and more. You may check the schedule of events on the Internet or at the box office. The location is Calle Acera del Casino 7, 18009 Granada, and the phone number is 958 22 13 11.

Teatro Alhambra: This theater is one of the most contemporary and inventive in Granada, situated in the Realejo area. It has a capacity of 400 seats and a modern design. It features events centered on contemporary invention and experimentation, such as dance, circus, puppetry, and more. Check the schedule of events on the Internet or at the box office. The location is Calle Molinos 56, 18009 Granada, and the phone number is 958 02 58 00.

Teatro Municipal José Tamayo: This theater is one of the most popular and accessible in Granada in the Zaidín district. It has a capacity of 300 seats and a comfortable aesthetic. It features events for a large audience, such as children's theater, comedy, magic, and more. You may check the schedule of events on the Internet or at the box office. The location is Calle Primavera s/n, 18008 Granada, and the phone number is 958 13 18 10.

Theaters Granada offers a range of theaters that provide diverse possibilities for movie enthusiasts, such as popular blockbusters, indie films, original versions, or 3D screenings. Some of the top cinemas in Granada are:

Cine Madrigal: This cinema is one of the most classic and attractive in Granada, situated on Calle Carrera de la Virgen. It contains one screen with a capacity of 500 seats and an old-fashioned appearance. It plays mostly Spanish and European films in their original language with subtitles. The location is Calle Carrera de la Virgen 14-16, 18005 Granada, and the phone number is 958 22 43 48.

Theater Andalucía 2000: This theater is one of the most contemporary and pleasant in Granada, situated in the Andalucía 2000 retail area. It includes eight screens with a total capacity of 1,600 seats and state-of-the-art technology. It broadcasts mostly Hollywood films dubbed in Spanish or with subtitles. You may check the program of films on the website https://www.andalucia.com/cities/granada/cinema.htm or at the ticket office. The location is Calle Arabial s/n (Centro

Comercial Andalucía), 18004 Granada, and the phone number is 958 52 28 48.

Kinepolis Granada: This cinema is one of the most magnificent and complete in Granada, situated in the Kinépolis retail park. It contains 15 screens with a total capacity of 4,500 seats and cutting-edge technology. It broadcasts all sorts of films in Spanish or original language with subtitles. It has additional amenities like restaurants, bars, shopping, and gaming. The location is Parque Comercial Kinépolis (Pulianas), and the phone number is 958 18 90 00.

We hope this chapter has given you valuable information and advice for your vacation to Granada. Granada is a city that will amaze you with its fun and entertainment alternatives, providing something for everyone. Whether you want to watch a performance or a movie, you will find a space that fits you. Enjoy your stay!

CHAPTER 5

Nature and Adventure

Granada is a city that will excite you with its environment and adventure options. Spectacular surroundings, such as the Sierra Nevada mountains, the Rio Verde Valley, and the Los Cahorros Canyon border it. You will discover activities that fit your tastes, whether you are searching for hiking, biking, skiing, canyoning, or more.

The city has a fortunate position and a diversified environment. It is located at the foot of the Sierra Nevada, the highest mountain range in Spain and one of the most popular places for skiing and snowboarding in Europe. It is also adjacent to the Tropical Coast, a beach resort with a warm temperature and a range of water activities. It is also home to various natural parks and reserves, where you may appreciate the flora and wildlife of Andalusia.

In this travel guide, you will discover all the information you need to explore and experience the finest of Granada's nature and adventure. You will learn about the greatest spots and regions to explore Granada's natural beauty and variety. You will also discover ideas and suggestions on preparing for your journey, what to pack, and what to anticipate.

The Sierra Nevada: a paradise for hikers and skiers

Granada is a city that provides a distinct contrast between the urban and the natural, between the antique and the contemporary, and between the warm and the cold. Granada is a city surrounded by the Sierra Nevada, the highest mountain range in mainland Spain and one of the most biodiverse locations in Europe. The Sierra Nevada is a paradise for hikers, skiers, and anybody who loves nature and adventure. In this chapter, you will discover the beauty and richness of the Sierra Nevada, its flora and fauna, its history and culture, its activities and its attractions.

You will also learn about the best methods to explore and appreciate the Sierra Nevada and some advice and ideas on how to prepare for your trip. Whether you are searching for a peaceful or demanding experience, a summer or a winter vacation, or a day or a week adventure, the Sierra Nevada offers something for you.

The Sierra Nevada is a mountain range that encompasses an area of around 2,000 square kilometers, ranging from Granada to Almería. It features 24 summits over 3,000 meters high, including Mulhacén (3,479 meters), the highest mountain in mainland Spain, and Veleta (3,396 meters), the second highest. The Sierra Nevada is part of the Penibaetic System, a geological structure that returns to the Paleozoic epoch. The Sierra Nevada is also part of the Sierra Nevada National Park, which was proclaimed a UNESCO Biosphere Reserve in 1986 and a World Heritage Site in 1999.

The Sierra Nevada is home to more than 2,100 plant species, of which 66 are endemic, meaning they are exclusively found in this region. The Sierra Nevada features a range of ecosystems, such as forests, meadows, wetlands and glaciers, that produce various habitats for different species. Some of the most distinctive flora of the Sierra Nevada are:

The Spanish fir (Abies pinsapo): A coniferous tree that thrives in the damp and shaded parts of the Sierra Nevada. It has dark green needles and cones that may grow up to 20 cm long. It is an endangered species that is protected by law.

The mountain violet (Viola crassiuscula): A little flower that grows in the rocky terrain of the high elevations of the Sierra Nevada. It features purple flowers and yellow stamens that contrast with its green foliage. It is one of the icons of the Sierra Nevada.

The snow star (Plantago nivalis): A herbaceous plant that thrives in the snowfields and glaciers of the Sierra Nevada. It has white blooms and thick leaves that endure cold temperatures and heavy winds. It is also an endemic and endangered species.

The Sierra Nevada is also home to more than 300 animal species, including mammals, birds, reptiles, amphibians and insects. The Sierra Nevada boasts a diverse fauna that adapts to the varied conditions and seasons of the mountain range. Some of the most distinctive creatures of the Sierra Nevada are:

The Spanish ibex (Capra pyrenaica): A wild goat living in the Sierra Nevada's mountainous parts. It has curving horns that may grow up to 80 cm long and a brown coat that varies according to the season. It is an agile and gregarious mammal that creates herds of up to 100 individuals.

The golden eagle (Aquila chrysaetos): A huge bird of prey that soars above the Sierra Nevada. It has dark brown feathers with golden hues on its head and neck. It has a wingspan of up to 2 meters and can attain speeds of up to 200 kilometers per hour. It feeds on rabbits, rats and other birds.

The Pyrenean desman (Galemys pyrenaicus): A tiny water animal that dwells in the rivers and streams of the Sierra Nevada. It has a large snout, webbed feet and a scaly tail that helps it swim and grab food. It feeds on insects, worms and crustaceans. It is an indigenous and endangered species.

The Sierra Nevada is not just a natural beauty but also a cultural treasure. The Sierra Nevada has been inhabited by many civilizations from ancient times, leaving behind traces of their history, culture and customs. Some of the most noteworthy cultural attractions of the Sierra Nevada are:

The Alpujarra: A area that encompasses the southern slopes of the Sierra Nevada, between Granada and Almería. It is notable for its white villages, like Lanjarón, Órgiva, Pampaneira or Trevélez, that maintain its Moorish architecture, culture and cuisine. The Alpujarra is also recognized for its handicrafts, including ceramics, carpets, baskets and ham. You can explore the Alpujarra by vehicle, bus or bike and enjoy its stunning scenery, quaint towns and wonderful gastronomy.

The Sulayr Route: A hiking track around the edge of the Sierra Nevada, spanning roughly 300 kilometers. It is separated into 19 stages, each with a distinct difficulty level, length and scenery. The Sulayr Route is named from the Arabic term for "mountain of the sun," which the Moors called the Sierra Nevada. You may walk the Sulayr Route by yourself or with a guide and enjoy the natural and cultural richness of the Sierra Nevada.

The Sierra Nevada Ski Resort: A ski resort on the northern slopes of the Sierra Nevada near Pradollano. It is Europe's highest and southernmost ski resort, with a height between 2,100 and 3,300 meters. It boasts more than 100 kilometers of ski slopes, appropriate for all abilities of skiers and snowboarders. It also offers various amenities and services, such as ski schools, equipment rental, restaurants and motels. You may ski at the Sierra Nevada Ski Resort from November to May and enjoy excellent snow quality, bright weather and spectacular vistas.

The Sierra Nevada is a paradise for hikers, skiers, and anybody who loves nature and adventure. This site will give you a choice of activities and attractions suited for all ages and interests. It is a location that will push, inspire, and reward you.

The Tropical Coast: a beach retreat near Granada

If you want a change of scenery and a pleasant escape from the city, you might try visiting the Tropical Coast, a coastline approximately an hour's drive south of Granada. The Tropical Coast is called by its moderate and sunny environment, which permits the development of exotic crops such as mangoes, avocados, and bananas. It is also noted for its stunning beaches, picturesque towns, and natural features. Whether you are searching for sun, water, sand, or adventure, the Tropical Coast provides something for everyone. Here are some of the top spots to visit on the Tropical Coast in 2023-2024:

Almuñécar: This is the biggest and most popular resort town on the Tropical Coast, with a history that stretches back to the Phoenicians. It boasts a bustling and cosmopolitan ambiance, with various stores, restaurants, bars, and nightlife alternatives. It also boasts a significant cultural past, including structures like the Castle of San Miguel, the Roman Aqueduct, and the Archaeological Museum. You may also enjoy some of its natural features, such as the Peñón del Santo (a rock formation that gives panoramic views), the Parque Botánico El Majuelo (a botanical garden with unusual plants), and the Parque Ornitológico Loro Sexi (a bird park with more than 1,500 species). Almuñécar is also famed for its beaches, which vary from sandy to rocky and from urban to remote. Some popular ones include San Cristóbal, Velilla, Puerta del Mar, and La Herradura. Almuñécar is a nice destination to enjoy the sun and the water on the Tropical Coast.

Salobreña: This is a gorgeous and attractive hamlet on a hilltop overlooking the Mediterranean Sea. It boasts a whitewashed and maze-like old town, with small streets and alleyways that lead to the Moorish Castle, which dominates the skyline. You may also visit some of its churches, such as the Iglesia de Nuestra Señora del Rosario or the Iglesia de San Juan Bautista. You may also enjoy some of its beaches, such as La Guardia or La Charca. Salobreña is an excellent destination to explore the history and culture of the Tropical Coast.

Motril: This is the second biggest town on the Tropical Coast and the area's primary economic and industrial hub. It has a contemporary and dynamic character, with a bustling harbor, a golf course, and a retail center. It also offers some of the greatest seafood restaurants on the coast, where you can experience the day's fresh catch. You can also visit some of its attractions, such as the Sugar Museum (a former sugar factory that displays the history and production of sugar cane), the Pre-Industrial Museum (a collection of old machines and tools), or the Sanctuary of Nuestra Señora de la Cabeza (a 17th-century church that hosts an annual pilgrimage). You may also enjoy some of its beaches, such as Playa Granada or Playa Poniente. Motril is an excellent destination to explore the modernity and variety of the Tropical Coast.

Nerja: This is a wonderful and attractive town situated on the eastern extremity of the Tropical Coast. It boasts a charming old town with whitewashed homes, flower-filled balconies, and quiet squares. It also features a stunning coastline, including cliffs, coves, and beaches. You can visit some of its attractions, such as the Balcony of Europe (a promenade that offers stunning views of the sea and the mountains), the Caves of Nerja (a natural wonder that contains prehistoric paintings and formations), or the Aqueduct of El Aguila (a 19th-century engineering masterpiece that supplied water to the sugar mills). You may also enjoy some of its beaches, such as Burriana, Torrecilla, or Maro. Nerja is a terrific destination to appreciate the beauty and charm of the Tropical Coast.

Almuñécar: This is the biggest and most popular resort town on the Tropical Coast, with a history that stretches back to the Phoenicians. It boasts a bustling and cosmopolitan ambiance, with various stores, restaurants, bars, and nightlife alternatives. It also boasts a significant cultural past, including structures like the Castle of San Miguel, the Roman Aqueduct, and the Archaeological Museum. You may also enjoy some of its natural features, such as the Peñón del Santo (a rock formation that gives panoramic views), the Parque Botánico El Majuelo (a botanical garden with unusual plants), and the Parque Ornitológico Loro Sexi (a bird park with more than 1,500 species). Almuñécar is also famed for its beaches, which vary from sandy to rocky and urban to remote. Some popular ones include San Cristóbal, Velilla, Puerta del Mar, and La Herradura. Almuñécar is a nice destination to enjoy the sun and the water on the Tropical Coast.

The Tropical Coast: a beach retreat near Granada (conclusion)

The Tropical Coast is a spot that will provide a calm and pleasurable escape from the city. It is a spot where you may enjoy the calm and sunny climate, the magnificent beaches, the attractive towns, and the natural attractions. It is also a site to enjoy fresh and tasty fish, unusual fruits, and local delicacies. The Tropical shore is a site where you may explore the richness and beauty of the shore near Granada.

The Alpujarras: a rustic getaway amid the mountains

Granada is a city that provides numerous attractions and activities for tourists, but occasionally you may leave the noise and bustle and enjoy more tranquil and natural surroundings. If so, consider visiting the Alpujarras, an area of mountains and valleys from the south of Granada to the east of Almeria.

The Alpujarras is a destination that will fascinate you with its beauty, history, and culture. It is a place where you can admire the stunning views of the Sierra Nevada, the highest mountain range in Spain; where you can explore the charming villages that preserve the architecture and traditions of the Moorish past; where you can taste the delicious cuisine that combines the influences of the Mediterranean and the mountains; and where you can experience the hospitality and warmth of the local people.

In this chapter, we will introduce you to some of the key sights and activities in the Alpujarras and some of the finest locations to stay and dine at. We will also offer suggestions on how to get there and make the most of your vacation.

Attractions

The Alpujarras offers several attractions for travelers who seek to learn about its history, culture, and environment. Here are some of the important ones:

The White Towns: The Alpujarras is famed for its white towns or pueblos blancos that dot the landscape with whitewashed buildings, flat roofs, and chimneys. These communities were created by the Moors, who arrived in the area after being ousted from Granada in 1492. They adapted to the hilly environment and produced a distinctive form of building that symbolizes their culture and personality. Some of the most attractive and charming settlements in the Alpujarras include Lanjarón, Órgiva, Pampaneira, Bubión, Capileira, Trevélez, Pitres, Pórtugos, Busquístar, La Taha, Mecina Bombarón, Yegen, Valor, Ugíjar, and Fondón.

The Poqueira Gorge: The Poqueira Gorge is one of the most stunning natural attractions in the Alpujarras. It is a steep ravine that runs along the Poqueira River, generating waterfalls, pools, and rapids. The gorge is also home to three of the most renowned white villages: Pampaneira, Bubión, and Capileira. These communities provide spectacular views of the canyon and the Sierra Nevada and intriguing attractions like museums, churches, artisan stores, and hiking routes.

The Mulhacén: The Mulhacén is the highest peak in Spain and continental Europe outside the Caucasus Mountains. It has a height of 3,479 meters (11,414 feet) and is part of the Sierra Nevada National Park. The Mulhacén is a popular location for mountaineers and hikers who wish to push themselves and enjoy the spectacular environment. There are various paths to reach the peak, but they all demand considerable fitness and expertise. The simplest and most accessible path is from Capileira to the Refugio Poqueira (a mountain hut), which takes around two days round trip.

The Alpujarra Museum: The Alpujarra Museum is a museum that highlights the history and culture of the Alpujarras. It is situated in Ugíjar, one of the main towns in the area. The museum features numerous halls that show exhibits on themes such as agriculture, crafts, textiles, ceramics, cuisine, religion, folklore, and literature. The museum also conducts guided tours, seminars, and events annually.

Activities

The Alpujarras provides various activities for people that wish to appreciate its environment and adventure. Here are some of the important ones:

Hiking: Hiking is one of the greatest ways to discover and enjoy the Alpujarras. Several hiking paths fit varying degrees of effort and time. Some of the more popular ones are:

The GR-7: This long-distance path spans Spain from east to west. It runs through the Alpujarras from Lanjarón to Cádiar, spanning roughly 150 kilometers (93 miles) in 10 stages. It gives excellent views of

The Sulayr: This circular route encircles the Sierra Nevada mountain. It has a total length of 300 kilometers (186 miles) and may be broken into 19 stages. It travels through some of

The Sendero de las Acequias (The Irrigation Channel route): This is a small route that follows a historic irrigation system established by the Moors to irrigate their crops. It begins at Capileira and concludes in Bubión, covering roughly 5 kilometers (3 miles) in 2 hours. It provides a taste of the rural life and the agricultural history of the Alpujarras.

Skiing: Skiing is another sport that can be done in the Alpujarras, particularly in the winter months. The Sierra Nevada Ski Resort is situated around 40 kilometers (25 miles) from Granada and offers 124 slopes of varying levels and 21 ski lifts. It also includes services such as ski schools, equipment rental, restaurants, and hotels. The ski resort is open from November to May, depending on the snow conditions.

Horse riding: Horse riding is a wonderful and peaceful way to experience the Alpujarras. Various horse riding facilities provide trips and excursions for all ages and levels. Some of the most recommended ones are Caballo Blanco in Lanjarón, Cabalgar Rutas Alternativas in Bubión, and Equiocio in Cádiar. You may pick from numerous routes that will take you via the white villages, the Poqueira Gorge, the Sierra Nevada, or the Mediterranean shore.

Cycling: Cycling is another alternative for people who wish to appreciate the Alpujarras on two wheels. Several bicycle routes vary from simple to tough, depending on the terrain and the distance. Some of the more popular ones are:

The Vía Verde de la Sierra Nevada (The Greenway of the Sierra Nevada): This bicycle path follows an ancient railway line that linked Granada with Almeria. It has a length of 34 km (21 miles) and travels via tunnels, bridges, and viaducts. It gives excellent views of the following:

The Ruta de los Pueblos Blancos (The path of the White settlements): This cycling path links some of the most stunning white settlements in the Alpujarras. It has a length of 60 km (37 miles) and travels via Lanjarón, Órgiva, Pampaneira, Bubión, Capileira, Trevélez, Pórtugos, Busquístar, La Taha, and Pitres.

The Ruta del Mulhacén (The path of the Mulhacén): This cycling path rises to the highest point in Spain and in continental Europe outside of the Caucasus Mountains. It has a length of 80 kilometers (50 miles) and begins at Capileira. It demands a high degree of fitness, expertise, and a mountain bike.

Places to stay

The Alpujarras provides a range of places to stay that appeal to various budgets and interests. You may select among hotels, hostels, guesthouses, flats, cottages, or campsites. Here are some of the greatest locations to stay in the Alpujarras:

Hotel Alcadima: This is a four-star hotel situated in Lanjarón, one of the principal towns in the Alpujarras. It features 30 rooms with balconies or terraces that give views of the mountains or the garden. It also features amenities such as a restaurant, a bar, a swimming pool, a spa, a sauna, a gym, and a tennis court.

Hostal Rural Poqueira: This is a two-star hostel in Capileira, one of the highest communities in the Alpujarras. It contains 19 rooms with private bathrooms and heaters. It also features amenities such as a restaurant, a bar, a balcony, and a lounge.

Casa Rural El Paraje: This is a rural guesthouse situated in Bérchules, one of the most isolated communities in the Alpujarras. It includes 6 rooms with private bathrooms and mountain views. It also features amenities such as a dining room, a kitchen, a garden, and a barbeque area.

Apartamentos Balcon del Cielo: These are flats situated in Trevélez, one of the highest and coldest communities in Spain. They offer 1 or 2 bedrooms with individual bathrooms and fireplaces. They also feature conveniences such as a kitchenette, a living room, a balcony or patio, and free WiFi.

Cortijo La Loma de la Alpujarra: This cottage is situated in Pitres, one of the main settlements in the Alpujarras. It offers 3 bedrooms with private baths and heaters. It also provides conveniences such as a kitchen, a living room, a fireplace, a terrace, and free WiFi.

Camping Los Bermejales: This is a campground situated in Arenas del Rey, near the Bermejales reservoir. It contains 60 spaces for tents, caravans, motorhomes, and 10 wooden cottages. It also features services such as a restaurant, a bar, a shop, a swimming pool, a playground, and a sports area.

Places to eat

The Alpujarras offers a rich and diverse cuisine that reflects its terrain and history. It mixes the influences of the Mediterranean and the Alps and the Moorish and Christian civilizations. Some of the characteristic foods of the Alpujarras are:

Plato alpujarreño: This is a robust meal that comprises fried potatoes, eggs, peppers, ham, sausage, and black pudding. It is frequently served with bread and wine.

Jamón de Trevélez: This is a cured ham created in Trevélez, one of the highest communities in Spain. It has a peculiar taste and scent due to the cold and dry atmosphere and the natural herbs used in its manufacture.

Migas: This dish is cooked from bread crumbs, garlic, oil, and water. It is generally paired with grapes, melon, sardines, or chorizo.

Puchero de Hinojosa: This stew is created with fennel, potatoes, chickpeas, pork ribs, and saffron. It is frequently served with bread and wine.

Sopa de almendras: This soup is created with almonds, garlic, bread, oil, vinegar, and water. It is normally served cold in the summer or heated in the winter.

Pestiños: These are pastries that are created with flour, oil, aniseed, and honey. They are commonly consumed at Easter or Christmas.

Some of the greatest places to eat in the Alpujarras are:

Mesón La Fragua: This is a classic restaurant situated in Trevélez. It provides a range of meals created with local goods, such as Plato alpujarreño, jamón de Trevélez, cheese, lamb, or fish. It also features a patio with views of the mountains.

Restaurante El Puente: This is a family-run restaurant situated in Pórtugos. It provides innovative and seasonal cuisine based on organic and ecological materials. Some of its highlights include migas with chocolate (bread crumbs with chocolate), puchero de hinojos con naranja (fennel stew with orange), or sopa de almendras con helado de Romero (almond soup with rosemary ice cream).

Pub El Chorro: This charming and friendly pub in Capileira. It provides a broad assortment of tapas and raciones (bigger servings) cooked using fresh and quality goods. Some of its specialities include croquetas de jamón (ham croquettes), ensalada de queso de cabra (goat cheese salad), or solomillo al Pedro Ximénez (pork tenderloin with Pedro Ximénez wine sauce).

Casa Diego: This is a bakery and pastry store situated in Bubión. It provides a range of breads and pastries created using natural and artisanal processes. Some of its delicacies include pan de higo (fig bread), rosquillas de anís (aniseed doughnuts), or pestiños.

How to get there

The Alpujarras is readily accessible from Granada by several kinds of transportation. Here are some of the major options:

By driving: The Alpujarras may be accessed by car through many highways that link Granada with the different cities and villages in the area. The key ones are:

The A-44/E-902: This roadway runs from Granada to Motril on the seashore. It has various exits that go to the Alpujarras, such as Lanjarón (exit 164), Órgiva (exit 175), or Vélez de Benaudalla (exit 187).

The A-348: This route travels from Lanjarón to Almeria in the heart of the Alpujarras. It travels through some of

The A-4132: This route travels from Órgiva to Trevélez via the Poqueira Gorge. It travels through some of

The A-337: This route travels from La Calahorra to Cádiar across the eastern section of the Alpujarras. It travels through some of

By bus: The Alpujarras may also be visited by bus from Granada. Bus companies operate frequent trips to the different cities and villages in the area, such as ALSA, Autocares José González, or Autocares Bonal. The bus station in Granada is situated on Avenida de Juan Pablo II, near the railway station. The bus costs and timetables vary based on the location and the season, but they are typically reasonable and convenient.

By taxi: The Alpujarras may also be visited by taxi from Granada. Various taxi companies provide services to the different cities and villages in the area, such as Radio Taxi Granada, Taxi Granada, or Taxi Alpujarra. The taxi costs and availability vary on the distance and the demand, but they are normally more costly and less frequent than the bus.

This chapter has given you an insight into the Alpujarras: a rural getaway in the mountains. We encourage you to visit this area and experience its beauty, history, and culture. We are confident you will enjoy a calm and gratifying time.

The Guadix Cave Houses: a unique experience in the desert

If you are seeking a unique and remarkable experience in Granada, you should visit the Guadix Cave Houses, a fascinating and traditional method of living in peace with nature. The Guadix Cave Houses are situated in the town of Guadix, approximately an hour's drive from Granada, amid the desert-like scenery of the Hoya de Guadix. This region is notable for its distinctive geological formations, such as the badlands, the clay hills, and the ravines. The cave dwellings are built into these hills, creating a bizarre and breathtaking backdrop.

The cave dwellings date back to the Roman era when the first residents scooped out the soft clay to make shelters from the severe weather conditions. The caverns were eventually occupied by the Moors, who built additional apartments and ornamentation. After the Christian reconquest, the caverns were abandoned by many of its residents, who relocated to more contemporary dwellings. However, some stayed in the caverns, retaining their ancient lifestyle and culture. Today, there are over 2,000 cave dwellings in Guadix, and residents still occupy half of them. The other half are utilized as tourist lodgings, museums, or cultural institutions.

The cave dwellings are not only a historical and cultural attraction but also an ecological and sustainable one. The caverns have natural insulation that keeps them cool in summer and warm in winter, avoiding the need for artificial heating or cooling. The caverns also feature a natural ventilation system that avoids dampness and mildew. The caverns have whitewashed walls, colorful tiles, wooden furnishings, and rustic accents. They feature all the contemporary facilities, such as power, water, internet, and restrooms. Some of them even have fireplaces, jacuzzis, or swimming pools.

The cave houses offer a unique opportunity to experience the authentic and traditional life of Guadix and enjoy the stunning views of the surrounding landscape. You can also explore the town of Guadix, which has many other attractions, such as the Cathedral, the castle, the Roman theater, and the pottery workshops. You can also visit the Purullena or Benalúa de Guadix villages, which have more cave houses and museums. You can also participate in hiking, biking, horse riding, or balloon flights.

The Guadix Cave Houses are a place that will surprise you with their beauty, charm, and comfort. They are a site that will make you feel closer to nature and history. They are a location that will provide you with a wonderful experience in Granada.

CHAPTER 6

Accommodation

Accommodation: finest hotels, hotels with addresses, websites and phone numbers on accommodation for travelers

Granada is a city that fascinates you with its history, culture, and beauty. But it will also give you a vast selection of housing alternatives where you may discover comfort, convenience, and elegance. Whether you are searching for a cheap hostel, a comfortable guesthouse, a luxury hotel, or a historic castle, Granada offers something for every taste and budget. Here are some of the greatest hotels, hotels with addresses, websites and phone numbers for lodgings for travelers in Granada in 2023-2024:

Eurostars Puerta Real: This is a contemporary 4-star hotel with excellent décor, situated in the city of Granada. Enjoy panoramic views from the rooftop bar. The sauna, gym and Turkish bath are an extra benefit. The rooms are big and beautiful, with air conditioning, heating, free WiFi, flat-screen TV, minibar, safe, and private bathroom. Some rooms additionally include a balcony or patio. The hotel provides a daily breakfast buffet that includes goods for celiacs. The hotel also offers a Mediterranean cuisine restaurant and a 24-hour reception to assist you with vehicle rentals, tickets, and excursions. The hotel is near the Cathedral, the Royal Chapel, and the Alcaicería market. It is also well linked by public transit to sights like the Alhambra or the Albaicín—a nice spot to enjoy some excellent service and amenities in Granada.

- Address: Calle Acera del Darro 24, 18005 Granada
- Phone number: +34 958 21 61 61 Website: Eurostars Puerta Real

Hotel Casa Morisca: This is a spectacular 15th-century aristocratic mansion restored to its former splendor. It is in the old Moorish area called the Albaicín, directly near the Darro River. It is one of the closest hotels to the Alhambra palace-fortress, which you can enjoy from some apartments or the patio. The rooms are furnished with exceptional elegance, blending classic features like wooden beams, tiles, arches, and fountains with contemporary facilities such as air conditioning, heating, free WiFi, flat-screen TV, minibar, safe, and private bathroom. Some rooms additionally feature a jacuzzi or a fireplace. The hotel provides a continental breakfast that may be served in your room or on the balcony. The hotel also features a lounge where you can relax and have tea or coffee. The hotel is situated near some of the most characteristic landmarks of Granada, such as the Paseo de los Tristes, the Plaza Nueva, or the Mirador de San Nicolás. An excellent site to explore the atmosphere and beauty of the old Granada.

- Address: Cuesta de la Victoria 9, 18010 Granada
- Phone number: +34 958 22 11 08 Website: Hotel Casa Morisca

Hotel Alhambra Palace: This is a luxury 5-star hotel that is nestled within the Alhambra complex, affording spectacular views of the city and the mountains. It is one of Spain's oldest and most prominent hotels, with a history that goes back to 1910. It features a grand and beautiful style, combining Moorish and classical inspirations. The rooms are big and pleasant, with air conditioning, heating, free WiFi, flat-screen TV, minibar, safe, and private bathroom. Some rooms additionally include a balcony or patio. The hotel serves a buffet breakfast that comprises local and foreign specialties. The hotel also boasts a restaurant with Mediterranean and Andalusian cuisine, a bar with drinks and live music, and a terrace with panoramic views. The hotel also features a 24-hour reception to assist you with tickets, excursions, and transportation. The hotel is near some of Granada's great attractions, such as the Alhambra Palace, the Generalife Gardens, and the Charles V Palace. An excellent spot to experience some luxury and exclusivity in Granada.

- Address: Plaza Arquitecto García de Paredes 1, 18009 Granada
- Phone number: +34 958 22 14 68

Hotel Casa 1800 Granada: This is a lovely 3-star hotel that is housed in a 16th-century home in the center of the Albaicín. It features a pleasant and romantic ambiance, with hardwood flooring, stone walls, and antique furniture. The rooms are pleasant and beautiful, with air conditioning, heating, free WiFi, flat-screen TV, minibar, safe, and private bathroom. Some rooms additionally feature a jacuzzi or a balcony. The hotel serves a complimentary afternoon tea, including coffee, juice, pastries, and fruit. The hotel also features a rooftop patio with excellent views of Alhambra and the city. The hotel also features a 24-hour desk to assist you with vehicle rental, laundry, and massage services. The hotel is situated near some of the most characteristic landmarks of Granada, such as the Paseo de los Tristes, the Plaza Nueva, or the Mirador de San Nicolás. An excellent spot to appreciate the elegance and tranquillity of the old Granada.

- Address: Calle Benalúa 11, 18010 Granada
- Phone number: +34 958 21 01 80

Hotel Palacio de Santa Paula: This is a luxury 5-star hotel that is set in a 16th-century convent and a 14th-century palace in the middle of Granada. It has a gorgeous and elegant style, with unique characteristics such as arches, courtyards, frescoes, and paintings. The rooms are big and pleasant, with air conditioning, heating, free WiFi, flat-screen TV, minibar, safe, and private bathroom. Some rooms additionally include a balcony or patio. The hotel serves a buffet breakfast that comprises local and foreign specialties. The hotel also boasts a restaurant that serves traditional Andalusian cuisine in a magnificent abbey, a bar that provides beverages and nibbles in a quiet lounge, and a spa that offers massages and treatments in a calm ambiance. The hotel also features a 24-hour reception to assist you with tickets, excursions, and transportation. The hotel is near some of Granada's great attractions, such as the Cathedral, the Royal Chapel, and the Alcaicería market. It is also well linked by public transit to sights like the Alhambra or the Albaicín—an excellent spot to spend some elegance and history in Granada.

Address: Calle Gran Vía de Colón 31, 18001 Granada Phone number: +34 958 80 57 40 Website: [Hotel Palacio de Santa Paula]

Hotel Carmen de la Alcubilla del Caracol: This is a lovely 3-star hotel that is housed in a 19th-century mansion on the slope of Alhambra Hill. It features a pleasant and romantic ambiance, with hardwood flooring, stone walls, and antique furniture. The rooms are pleasant and beautiful, with air conditioning, heating, free WiFi, flat-screen TV, minibar, safe, and private bathroom. Some rooms additionally feature a jacuzzi or a fireplace. The hotel provides a continental breakfast that may be served in your room or on the balcony. The hotel also includes a garden where you can rest and enjoy the views of Alhambra and the city. The hotel also features a 24-hour desk to assist you with vehicle rental, laundry, and massage services. The hotel is situated near some of the most characteristic landmarks of Granada, such as the Paseo de los Tristes, the Plaza Nueva, or the Mirador de San Nicolás. An excellent spot to appreciate the elegance and tranquillity of the old Granada.

- Address: Calle Aire Alta 12, 18009 Granada
- Phone number: +34 958 22 64 90

Accommodation (conclusion)

Granada is a city that will give you a broad selection of hotel alternatives where you may find comfort, convenience, and elegance. Whether you are searching for a cheap hostel, a comfortable guesthouse, a luxury hotel, or a historic castle, Granada offers something for every taste and budget.

CHAPTER 7

3-7 Days Itinerary for Granada

Granada is a city that will fascinate you with its beauty and its mysteries. It offers much, from the magnificent Alhambra to the vibrant tapas restaurants, from the old Albayzín to the futuristic Science Park. You will need at least three days to visit the attractions of Granada, but you may also prolong your stay to discover more of its surroundings and culture.

In this travel guide, you will discover a recommended schedule for 3-7 days in Granada, depending on your time and what you want to accomplish. You will also discover ideas and suggestions for making the most of your vacation, such as where to stay, how to get about, and what to eat.

3 Days in Granada

If you only have three days in Granada, you should concentrate on the major attractions of the city center and the Alhambra complex. Here is a schedule for 3 days in Granada:

Day 1: Alhambra and Generalife

The Alhambra is the most renowned and spectacular attraction in Granada. It is a complex of palaces and gardens that was the seat of the Nasrid monarchs, the last Muslim rulers of Spain. It is a UNESCO World Heritage Site and one of the most visited destinations in the world.

The Alhambra is perched on a mountaintop overlooking the city and the mountains. It encompasses an area of around 13 hectares (32 acres) and comprises various buildings and structures, each with its purpose and design. The primary sections of the complex are:

The Alcazaba: the oldest and most defended portion of the Alhambra, which functioned as a military barracks and a watchtower. It provides magnificent views of Granada and the Sierra Nevada. You may climb to the top of the Torre de la Vela (Tower of the Candle), which was used to indicate the beginning and end of the day with a bell.

The Nasrid Palaces: the most magnificent and elegant component of the Alhambra, which functioned as the royal palace and court. They are separated into three sections: the

Mexuar, where administrative and judicial issues were managed; the Comares Palace, where formal banquets and ceremonies were held; and the Palace of the Lions, where private life and amusement took place. Each part has chambers, courtyards, hallways, and fountains covered with exquisite geometric designs, arabesques, calligraphy, tiles, stucco, and woodwork. Some of the more notable characteristics are:

- The Patio del Mexuar (Court of the Mexuar), with its porticoed gallery and its oratory niche facing Mecca.

- The Patio de los Arrayanes (Court of the Myrtles), with its long rectangular pool mirroring the exterior of the Comares Palace.

- The Sala de la Barca (Hall of the Boat), with its hardwood roof resembling an inverted boat hull.

- The Sala de los Embajadores (Hall of the Ambassadors), with its octagonal roof adorned with star-shaped patterns.

- The Patio de los Leones (Court of the Lions), with its famed fountain supported by twelve marble lions.

- The Sala de los Abencerrajes (Hall of the Abencerrages), with its stalactite dome and its narrative of horrific slaughter.

- The Sala de las Dos Hermanas (Hall of the Two Sisters), with its exquisite ceiling and its mirador (viewing window) overlooking the garden.

- The Sala de los Reyes (Hall of the Kings), with its painted leather ceiling showing hunting scenes.

The Palace of Charles V: a Renaissance-style palace erected by Charles V, Holy Roman Emperor and King of Spain, in 1526. It was meant to be his house in Granada, but it was never built or occupied. It contains a circular courtyard encircled by two floors of columns.

It contains two museums: the Museum of Fine Arts, which shows paintings and sculptures from the 15th to 20th centuries, and the Museum of Alhambra, which exhibits

Islamic art and relics from the Alhambra and other places in Granada.

The Generalife: a summer palace and gardens situated near the Alhambra. Muhammad III established it in the 14th century as a place to rest and appreciate nature. It contains multiple courtyards, pavilions, pools, fountains, flowers, and trees. Some of the highlights are:

- The Patio de la Acequia (Court of the Water Channel), with its long pool served by four jets and surrounded by flower gardens.

- The Patio de la Sultana (Court of the Sultana), with its cypress tree, where according to folklore, Boabdil's wife Zoraya met her lover.

- The Escalera del Agua (Stairway of Water) has stairs going along a wall with water pipes that give a pleasant impression.

- The Mirador Romántico (Romantic Viewpoint), with stunning views of the Alhambra and Granada.

To visit the Alhambra, you need to book your ticket online in advance since they sell out rapidly. You may pick between several sorts of tickets based on what you want to see and when you want to go. You may also take a guided tour explaining the history and importance of each section of the complex. You should expect to spend at least three hours to see everything, but you may certainly spend more time if you want to appreciate it at your speed.

The Alhambra site will astound you with its beauty and refinement. It is a destination that will transfer you to another period and culture. It is a site that will make you admire the art and architecture of the Islamic world. It is a spot that you will never forget.

After touring Alhambra, you may eat lunch at one of the neighboring restaurants or cafés, such as La Mimbre or La Chistera. You may sample several classic meals from Granada, such as habeas with jamón (fava beans with ham) or tortilla del Sacromonte (omelet with mutton brains).

Stroll down the Cuesta de Gomérez in the afternoon, a steep roadway from Alhambra to the city center. On your route, you may stop at numerous fascinating locations, such as:

- The Puerta de las Granadas (Gate of the Pomegranates) is a 16th-century gate that marks the entrance to the Alhambra complex. It contains three arches adorned with pomegranates, the emblem of Granada.

- The Plaza Nueva (New Plaza) is the oldest plaza in Granada and a gathering spot for residents and visitors. It contains a fountain, a monument of King Ferdinand and Queen Isabella, and various pubs and restaurants.

- The Iglesia de Santa Ana (Church of Saint Anne) is a 16th-century church erected on the site of a medieval mosque. It features a Mudejar tower, a Gothic gateway, and a Baroque interior.

- The Real Chancillería (Royal Chancellery) was a 16th-century building that was the site of Andalusia's highest court of law. It contains a Renaissance exterior, a courtyard with columns, and a staircase with paintings.

You may also cross the Darro River and explore the Carrera del Darro, one of the most gorgeous avenues in Granada. It goes along the riverbed and provides views of the Alhambra and the Albayzín. It has various historic structures, such as:

The Bañuelo (Arab Baths) is one of the oldest and finest maintained Arab baths in Spain. They date back to the 11th century and feature multiple chambers with vaulted ceilings and star-shaped skylights.

The Casa de Castril (Castril House) is a 16th-century house that was the home of Hernando de Zafra, the secretary of Queen Isabella. It features a Plateresque exterior, a courtyard with columns, and a balcony with ironwork. It holds the Archaeological Museum, which shows items from diverse eras and civilizations, including Roman, Visigothic, and Moorish.

The Casa de los Pisa (Pisa House), a 16th-century mansion that the Pisa family erected and that was subsequently dedicated to San Juan de Dios, one of Spain's major religious personalities. It has his antiquities, artwork, furnishings, and personal stuff.

You may conclude your day by eating supper at one of the numerous tapas bars in Granada, where you can enjoy complimentary tapas with your drink order. You may taste local delicacies, such as remojón granaíno (salad with cod, orange, and pomegranate) or olla de San Antón (stew with pig leftovers). You may also enjoy some live music or flamenco at several of the places in Granada, such as La Tertulia or La Chumbera. Granada is a city that boasts a dynamic and exciting nightlife, where you can have fun and meet new people.

Day 2: Albayzín and Sacromonte

The Albayzín is the historic Moorish neighborhood of Granada, which maintains its medieval layout and its whitewashed homes. It is also a UNESCO World Heritage Site and a spot where you can enjoy the greatest views of the Alhambra from the Mirador de San Nicolás. You will feel like you have been transported back in time as you meander through its small alleyways, secret squares, and historic mosques and churches.

The Sacromonte is the district where many gypsies dwell in cave homes dug into the mountainside. It is the cradle of flamenco, a passionate and expressive art style that mixes music, dancing, and singing. You will get the option to attend a flamenco concert in one of the cameras, tiny settings where you can experience the artists' passion and intensity.

To see the Albayzín and Sacromonte, you may take a bus or a cab from the city center or walk up the Cuesta del Chapiz, a hilly route that links them. You may also take a guided tour that will show you the most intriguing spots and explain the history and legends of these areas. You should expect to spend at least two hours to see everything, but you may also spend more time if you want to explore them at your leisure.

The Albayzín and Sacromonte are destinations that fascinate you with their atmosphere and culture. They are sites that will show you the variety and uniqueness of Granada. They are spots that will help you experience Granada's spirit and essence.

Some of the sites that you should not miss in the Albayzín and Sacromonte are:

- The Mirador de San Nicolás (Viewpoint of Saint Nicholas) plaza affords a spectacular perspective of the Alhambra, particularly around sunset. It is also a popular area for residents and visitors to hang out, perform music, or snap photographs.

- The Iglesia de San Nicolás (Church of Saint Nicholas) is a 16th-century church near the lookout. It contains a Mudejar tower, a Baroque exterior, and an interior with paintings and sculptures.

- The Mezquita Mayor de Granada (Great Mosque of Granada) is a mosque that was erected in 2003 as a symbol of tolerance and peace between Muslims and Christians in Granada. It contains a minaret, a courtyard, and a prayer hall with Arabic calligraphy and geometric elements.

- The Casa de Zafra (Zafra House) is a 14th-century mansion that was the seat of a rich merchant family. It contains a courtyard with columns, arches, and fountains and numerous rooms with exhibits on the history and culture of the Albayzín.

- The Palacio de Dar al-Horra (Palace of Dar al-Horra) was a 15th-century palace that was the abode of Aixa, Boabdil's mother and one of the most powerful ladies in Granada. It contains a courtyard with arcades, a tower with views of the Alhambra, and numerous apartments with unique décor.

- The Museo Arqueológico y Etnológico de Granada (Archaeological and Ethnological Museum of Granada) is a museum that shows items from diverse eras and civilizations, such as Roman, Visigothic, Moorish, Jewish, Christian, and Gypsy. It is housed in the Casa del Castril, a 16th-century mansion that was the home of Hernando de Zafra, the secretary of Queen Isabella.

- The Abadía del Sacromonte (Sacromonte monastery) is a 17th-century monastery that was established on the spot where certain remains of Saint Caecilius were recovered. It features a church, a cloister, and many chapels with paintings and sculptures. It also contains a museum showcasing some of the treasures, literature, coins, weapons, and clothing.

- The Cuevas del Sacromonte (Sacromonte Caves) are cave homes where many gypsies reside or rent to visitors. They are adorned with colorful textiles, ceramics, paintings, and other artifacts. They also have fireplaces, kitchens, and baths.

- The Zambras del Sacromonte (Sacromonte Zambras) are flamenco venues where you may witness true flamenco acts performed by gypsy performers. They are frequently placed in cave dwellings or in courtyards with tables and chairs. They serve beverages and occasionally meals.

After touring the Albayzín and Sacromonte, you may have lunch at one of the surrounding restaurants or cafés, such as El Trillo or El Huerto de Juan Ranas. You may sample some classic meals from Granada, such as Plato alpujarreño (a dish with potatoes, eggs, ham, sausage, and pepper) or tortilla del Sacromonte (an omelet with mutton brains).

In the afternoon, you may stroll along the Paseo de los Tristes, a promenade that runs along the Darro River and boasts views of the Alhambra and the Albayzín. On your route, you may stop at numerous fascinating locations, such as:

The Puente del Aljibillo (Aljibillo Bridge) is a 16th-century bridge that spans the Darro River. It features a stone arch with a wooden railing. It is also known as the Puente de las Chirimías (Bridge of the Shawms) since it was where musicians performed during festivals and festivities.

The Puerta de Elvira (Elvira Gate) is a 14th-century gate that was the principal entry to Granada during the Muslim era. It features a horseshoe arch and a tower with battlements. It is additionally embellished with ceramic tiles and Arabic inscriptions.

The Corral del Carbón (Coal Yard) is a 14th-century edifice that was used as a storehouse and a hostel for merchants. It contains a courtyard with a fountain and a gallery with arches. It also features a theater where cultural activities are hosted.

You may conclude your day by eating supper at one of the numerous tapas bars in Granada, where you can enjoy complimentary tapas with your drink order. You may taste local delicacies, such as remojón granaíno (salad with cod, orange, and pomegranate) or olla de San Antón (stew with pig leftovers). You may also enjoy some live music or flamenco at several places in Granada, such as La Tertulia or La Chumbera. Granada is a city that boasts a dynamic and exciting nightlife, where you can have fun and meet new people.

Day 3: City Center and Realejo

The city center of Granada is where you can discover some of the city's most notable monuments and structures, such as the Cathedral, the Royal Chapel, and the Madraza. It is also where you can find some of Granada's most popular streets and squares, such as the Calle Reyes Católicos, the Plaza Bib-Rambla, and the Calle Navas. You will love Granada's architecture and culture, as well as its shops and cafés.

The Realejo is the historic Jewish district of Granada, inhabited by Jews until their expulsion in 1492. It is today a bustling and colorful area where you can discover several noteworthy locations, such as the Campo del Príncipe, the Casa de los Tiros, and the Cuarto Real de Santo Domingo. You will also discover some street art by El Niño de las Pinturas, a prominent graffiti artist from Granada.

To access the city center and Realejo, you may walk from Plaza Nueva or take a bus or a cab from any place in Granada. You may also take a guided tour that will show you the most intriguing spots and explain the history and legends of these regions. You should expect to spend at least two hours to see everything, but you may also spend more time if you want to explore them at your leisure.

The city center and Realejo are areas that will wow you with their monuments and their atmosphere. They are locations that will show you Granada's history and identity. They are spots that will let you experience Granada's essence and spirit.

Some of the sites that you should not miss in the city center and Realejo are:

The Cathedral of Granada: This is one of Spain's biggest and most stunning cathedrals. It was erected between 1523 and 1704 on the site of a prior mosque. It features a Gothic foundation, a Renaissance front, and a Baroque interior. It features five naves, multiple chapels, an altar, an organ, and a dome. It also features paintings by Alonso Cano, Pedro de Mena sculptures, and Diego de Siloé tombs.

The Royal Chapel is where the Catholic Monarchs, Ferdinand and Isabella, are buried. They were the ones who seized Granada in 1492 and concluded the Reconquista, the centuries-long war between Christians and Muslims in Spain. They also funded Christopher Columbus's journey to America in 1492. Their beautiful graves are fashioned of marble and contain statues of them lying on top. They also have a vast collection of art and treasures, such as their crowns, swords, wands, and personal possessions.

The Madraza: This was the first university in Granada, created by Yusuf I in 1349. It was a center of study and culture where students studied disciplines like theology, law, medicine, and astronomy. It was also a worship center featuring a mosque and a prayer hall. After the Christian takeover, it was renovated into a town hall and a church. It still has some original characteristics, such as the wooden ceiling, the marble arch, and the mihrab (prayer niche).

The Calle Reyes Católicos (Street of the Catholic Monarchs): This is one of the major avenues of Granada, where you can find numerous stores, cafés, banks, and hotels. It was named after Ferdinand and Isabella, who invaded Granada along this street following their triumph in 1492. It also has various monuments and structures of importance, such as:

The Fuente de las Batallas (Fountain of the Wars) is a 17th-century fountain that honors the wars waged by the Catholic Monarchs during the Reconquista.

The Iglesia de San Gil y Santa Ana (Church of Saint Giles and Saint Anne) is a 16th-century church with a Mudejar tower, a Baroque gateway, and an interior with paintings and sculptures.

The Capilla Real (Royal Chapel) is a 16th-century chapel created by Charles V to expand the Cathedral. It has Gothic architecture and houses the graves of Ferdinand and Isabella's successors: Joanna the Mad, Philip the Handsome, and Miguel da Paz.

The Plaza Bib-Rambla (Bib-Rambla Square): This is one of the most popular squares in Granada, where you can find numerous flower sellers, cafés, restaurants, and street entertainers. It was once the location of a Moorish gate and market, where silk and spices were traded. It also has various historic structures, such as:

The Fuente de los Gigantes (Fountain of the Giants) is a 17th-century fountain that contains four sculptures depicting the four rivers of Paradise: Tigris, Euphrates, Nile, and Ganges.

The Iglesia de la Magdalena (Church of Mary Magdalene) a 16th-century church that contains a Mudejar tower, a Renaissance gateway, and an interior with paintings and sculptures.

The Casa de los Tiros (House of the Shots) a 16th-century mansion that features a façade with bullet holes during an insurrection in 1590. It contains the Museum of History and Culture of Granada, which shows items from many eras and parts of Granada's history and culture.

The Calle Navas (Navas Street): This is one of the greatest streets in Granada to savor tapas, little servings of food provided for free with your drink order. You may discover several taverns and restaurants that provide various tapas, such as cheese, ham, croquettes, meatballs, potatoes, fish, and more. You may also discover several dishes from Granada, such as remojón granaíno (salad with cod, orange, and pomegranate) or olla de San Antón (stew with pig leftovers).

The Realejo is the historic Jewish district of Granada, inhabited by Jews until their expulsion in 1492. It is today a bustling and colorful area where you can discover various fascinating sites, such as:

The Campo del Príncipe (Field of the Prince) was a square named after Prince Juan, the son of Ferdinand and Isabella, who died in 1497. It contains a fountain, a Cristo de los Favores (Christ of Favors) statue, and various pubs and restaurants. It is also a popular area for residents and visitors to hang out, perform music, or snap photographs.

The Casa de los Tiros (House of the Shots) a 16th-century mansion that features a façade with bullet holes during an insurrection in 1590. It contains the Museum of History and Culture of Granada, which shows items from many eras and parts of Granada's history and culture.

The Cuarto Real de Santo Domingo (Royal Quarter of Saint Dominic) is a 13th-century mansion Muhammad II erected as his vacation retreat. It contains a courtyard with arcades, a garden with fountains, and numerous rooms with unique décor. It also holds temporary exhibits and cultural activities.

After touring the city center and Realejo, you may have lunch at one of the neighboring restaurants or cafés, such as Los Diamantes or La Cuchara de Carmela. You may sample several classic meals from Granada, such as habas with jamón (fava beans with ham) or tortilla del Sacromonte (omelet with mutton brains).

In the afternoon, you may see some of the other attractions that Granada has to offer, such as:

The Science Park is an interactive and informative museum covering numerous aspects of science and technology. It features permanent and temporary displays, a planetarium, a butterfly house, an observation tower, and a tropical forest.

The Manuel de Falla House Museum: named for the Cádiz-born musician who became one of the most notable Spanish composers of the 20th century. It showcases his things, papers, instruments, and correspondence.

The Federico García Lorca House Museum: Situated in the Huerta de San Vicente park, this was the vacation house of Lorca's family and a key site in the creative production of this worldwide Spanish poet. It keeps his furnishings, books, sketches, and writings.

The Caja Granada Cultural Center: a contemporary and multipurpose venue that holds exhibits, concerts, seminars, conferences, and other cultural events. It contains a permanent exhibition on the history and culture of Andalusia, as well as a temporary exhibition on modern art.

You may conclude your day by eating supper at one of the numerous tapas bars in Granada, where you can enjoy complimentary tapas with your drink order. You may taste local delicacies, such as remojón granaíno (salad with cod, orange, and pomegranate) or olla de San Antón (stew with pig leftovers). You may also enjoy some live music or flamenco at several places in Granada, such as La Tertulia or La Chumbera. Granada is a city that boasts a dynamic and exciting nightlife, where you can have fun and meet new people.

4-7 Days in Granada

If you have more than three days in Granada, you might prolong your stay to see more of its surroundings and culture. Here are some recommendations for 4-7 days in Granada:

Day 4: Sierra Nevada

The Sierra Nevada is the tallest mountain range in Spain and one of Europe's most popular places for skiing and snowboarding. It offers nearly 100 kilometers of slopes, appropriate for all abilities of skiers and snowboarders. It also contains a national park encompassing more than 85,000 hectares of protected area, where you may discover different flora and animals, such as ibexes, eagles, and wildflowers. You may walk, ride, or join a 4WD safari excursion to explore the park.

To explore the Sierra Nevada, you may take a bus or a cab from Granada to Pradollano, the biggest ski resort in the region. You may hire a vehicle or join a guided trip to take you there. You should plan to spend at least four hours enjoying the snow and the outdoors, but you may also spend a longer time if you want to attempt new things.

The Sierra Nevada is a destination that will astound you with its beauty and uniqueness. It is a site that will give you a range of activities and experiences, from skiing to snowboarding, from hiking to riding. It is a spot that will let you experience nature's excitement and delight.

After viewing the Sierra Nevada, you may have lunch at one of the surrounding restaurants or cafés, such as La Antorcha or La Visera. You may sample classic foods from the highlands, such as migas (fried bread crumbs with garlic and sausage) or choto al ajillo (baby goat with garlic).

In the afternoon, you may explore some of the settlements in the Alpujarras, an area that spans along the southern slopes of the Sierra Nevada. They are lovely settlements that keep their Moorish architecture and culture, such as Lanjarón, Órgiva, Pampaneira, Bubión, Capileira, and Trevélez. You may appreciate their whitewashed buildings, terraced fields, water channels, and crafts. You may also try their goods, such as cheese, ham, honey, and wine.

You may conclude your day by eating supper at one of the numerous tapas bars in Granada, where you can enjoy complimentary tapas with your drink order. You may taste local delicacies, such as remojón granaíno (salad with cod, orange, and pomegranate) or olla de San Antón (stew with pig leftovers). You may also enjoy some live music or flamenco at several places in Granada, such as La Tertulia or La Chumbera.

Granada is a city that has a lot to offer, but you can also take some day excursions to other sites that are worth seeing. Here are some recommendations for 5-7 days in Granada:

Day 5: Córdoba

Córdoba is a city that was the capital of Muslim Spain and one of the most significant cultural centers of the globe. It has a rich and diversified past, including monuments and structures from many times and faiths. It is also a UNESCO World Heritage Site and a destination where you can appreciate Andalusia's art, food, and ambiance.

To reach Córdoba, take a train or a bus from Granada, which takes around two hours. You may hire a vehicle or join a guided trip to take you there. You should expect to spend at least six hours visiting the major attractions of Córdoba, but you may certainly spend more time if you want to explore it at your leisure.

Córdoba is a location that amazes you with its beauty and history. It is a location that will show you Muslim Spain's magnificence and collapse. It is a site that will make you appreciate Andalusia's serenity and variety.

Some of the sites that you should not miss in Córdoba are:

The Mezquita-Catedral (Mosque-Cathedral) is the most famous and spectacular attraction in Córdoba. It was erected between the 8th and the 10th centuries as a mosque and later renovated into a cathedral in the 16th century. It features a vast rectangular floor layout, with 19 naves and approximately 800 columns supporting horseshoe arches. It contains numerous parts, such as:

- The Patio de los Naranjos (Courtyard of the Orange Trees), where the ablutions (religious washing) were done before entering the mosque. It contains a fountain, orange trees, palm trees, and cypresses.

- The Mihrab (Prayer Niche) symbolizes the direction of Mecca and where the imam (prayer leader) stood. It features a dome with mosaics, marble, and gold.

- The Maqsura (Enclosure) was designated for the caliph and his court. It features a dome with stalactites and arches with geometric motifs.

- The Capilla Mayor (Main Chapel) was created in the heart of the mosque as part of the renovation into a cathedral. It features a Gothic style and comprises an altar, an organ, and a choir.

- The Capilla de Villaviciosa (Chapel of Villaviciosa) was one of the earliest components of the mosque and one of the few retained throughout the conversion. It features a dome with arabesques and inscriptions.

- Ferdinand III erected the Capilla Real (Royal Chapel) after he captured Córdoba in 1236. It includes his grave, his son Alfonso X, and his grandson Ferdinand IV.

- The Alcázar de los Reyes Cristianos (Alcazar of the Christian Monarchs) was a fortress-palace erected by Alfonso XI in 1328 on a medieval Muslim stronghold site. It was used as a house by Ferdinand III, Alfonso X, Ferdinand IV, Peter I, Henry II, John II, Henry IV, Isabella I, Ferdinand II, Charles V, Philip II, and Philip III. It also served as a jail for Christopher Columbus in 1500. It has numerous characteristics, such as:

- The Torre del Homenaje (Tower of Homage) is the tallest tower of the Alcazar and gives panoramic views of Córdoba.

- The Torre de los Leones (Tower of the Lions) is where Christopher Columbus was imprisoned and met with Ferdinand II and Isabella I to discuss his intentions for his expedition to America.

- The Salón de los Mosaicos (Hall of Mosaics) shows Roman mosaics from the 2nd and 3rd centuries uncovered in the Corredera plaza.

- The Christian rulers utilized the Baños Reales (Royal Baths) for their cleanliness and leisure. They have numerous rooms, such as the cold room, the warm room, the hot room, and the dressing room.

- The Jardines del Alcázar (Gardens of the Alcazar) is separated into three terraces with fountains, ponds, flowers, trees, and sculptures. They have numerous styles, such as the Islamic, Renaissance, and Baroque styles.

- The Judería (Jewish Quarter) is one of the most picturesque and bustling districts of Córdoba. Jews inhabited it until their deportation in 1492. It features tiny alleys, whitewashed cottages, courtyards, and stores. It also has various monuments and structures of importance, such as:

- The Sinagoga (Synagogue) was one of the only three synagogues that remained in Spain following the expulsion of the Jews. It was erected in 1315 and features Mudejar architecture. It contains a prayer hall with Hebrew calligraphy and geometric elements.

- The Casa de Sefarad (House of Sepharad) is a museum that showcases the history and culture of the Sephardic Jews, the descendants of the Jews who resided in Spain before 1492. It features numerous rooms with topics such as music, ladies, festivals, literature, and crafts.

- The Casa Andalusí (Andalusian home) is a home that recreates the ambiance and the lifestyle of a typical Andalusian residence from the 12th century. It contains a courtyard with a fountain, a garden with plants, and many rooms with furniture and items.

After touring Córdoba, you may eat lunch at one of the neighboring restaurants or cafés, such as Casa Pepe or Bodegas Campos. You may sample classic foods from Córdoba, such as salmorejo (cold tomato soup with bread, garlic, olive oil, and vinegar) or flamenquín (fried pig roll with ham and cheese).

In the afternoon, you may return to Granada, or you can remain in Córdoba to view some of the other things that Córdoba has to offer, such as:

The Puente Romano (Roman Bridge) is a bridge that spans the Guadalquivir River and links the city center with the Calahorra Tower. It was erected by the Romans in the 1st century BC and renovated by the Muslims in the 8th century. It contains 16 arches and a statue of Saint Raphael, the patron saint of Córdoba.

The Torre de la Calahorra (Calahorra Tower) is a defensive tower erected by the Muslims in the 12th century and rebuilt by the Christians in the 14th century. It contains the Museum of Andalusian Life, which portrays the history and culture of Andalusia from the 9th to the 15th century.

The Medina Azahara (Shining City) is a palace city created by Abd al-Rahman III in the 10th century as his home and capital. It was one of the most wealthy and sophisticated towns of its time, but it was destroyed by a civil war in 1010. It has been partly excavated and repaired and exhibits some of its original characteristics, such as walls, arches, columns, fountains, and gardens.

You may conclude your day by eating supper at one of the numerous tapas bars in Córdoba, where you can enjoy complimentary tapas with your drink order. You may taste local delicacies, such as berenjenas con miel (fried eggplant with honey) or rabo de toro (bull's tail stew). You may also enjoy live music or flamenco at several places in Córdoba, such as La Bulería or El Cardenal.

Day 6: Málaga

Málaga is a city on the Costa del Sol, a beach resort with a pleasant temperature and a range of water activities. It is also a city that has a rich and diversified legacy, including monuments and structures from many times and civilizations. It is also a city that boasts a dynamic and contemporary culture, including museums, festivals, and nightlife.

To reach Málaga, take a train or a bus from Granada, which takes around two hours. You may hire a vehicle or join a guided trip to take you there. You should expect to spend at least six hours visiting the major attractions of Málaga, but you may even spend more time if you want to explore it at your leisure.

Málaga is a location that amazes you with its beauty and variety. It is a site that will give you various experiences and activities, from sunbathing to surfing, from sightseeing to shopping. It is a location that will make you feel pleased and comfortable.

Some of the sites that you should not miss in Málaga are:

The Alcazaba is a fortress-palace erected by the Muslims in the 11th century on the site of an ancient Roman stronghold. It was used as a home by numerous Muslim kings until it was seized by Ferdinand II in 1487. It has numerous characteristics, such as:

The Puerta de las Columnas (Gate of Columns) is the principal entrance to the Alcazaba. It contains a horseshoe arch and two Roman columns repurposed from a neighboring theater. - The Patio de Armas (Courtyard of Arms), the first courtyard of the Alcazaba. It features a cistern, a well, and many towers. - The Patio de los Naranjos (Courtyard of the Orange Trees), the second courtyard of the Alcazaba. It contains a fountain, orange trees, and numerous chambers with arches and columns. - The Torre del Homenaje (Tower of Homage), the tallest tower of the Alcazaba, gives panoramic views of Málaga and the coastline.

The Castillo de Gibralfaro (Gibralfaro fortress) is a fortress that was erected by the Muslims in the 14th century on top of a hill that overlooks the city. It was utilized as a military fortification and a watchtower until it was ceded to Ferdinand II in 1487. It has numerous characteristics, such as:

- The Puerta de los Cuartos (Gate of the Quarters) is the primary entrance to the fortress. It features a double arch and a coat of arms of the Catholic Monarchs.

- The Patio de Armas (Courtyard of Arms) is the principal courtyard of the castle. It features a cistern, a well, and many barracks.

- The Torre Mayor (Major Tower) is the castle's tallest tower and gives panoramic views of Málaga and the Mediterranean.

- The Museo de la Cerámica y la Armería (Museum of Pottery and Armory) showcases pottery, weaponry, and uniforms from many times and civilizations.

- The Catedral de la Encarnación (Cathedral of the Incarnation) is popularly known as La Manquita (The One-Armed Lady) since one of its towers was never finished. It was erected between 1528 and 1782 on the site of a medieval mosque. It features a Renaissance style with Gothic, Baroque, and Neoclassical characteristics. It features three naves, multiple chapels, an altar, an organ, and a choir. It also features paintings by Alonso Cano, Pedro de Mena sculptures, and Diego de Siloé tombs.

- The Museo Picasso Málaga (Picasso Museum Málaga) is a museum that shows the works of Pablo Picasso, one of the most important painters of the

20th century and a native of Málaga. It comprises approximately 200 paintings, drawings, sculptures, ceramics, and prints spanning his career. It also includes temporary exhibits, workshops, talks, and performances.

- The Teatro Romano (Roman Theater) was a theater that was erected by the Romans in the 1st century BC and rediscovered in 1951. It contains an orchestra, a stage, and seating for 220 people. It also features a visitor center that shows various relics and information about its history and restoration.

After touring Málaga, you may eat lunch at one of the neighboring restaurants or cafés, such as El Pimpi or La Cosmopolitan. You may sample some classic meals from Málaga, such as espetos de sardinas (sardines skewered on sticks and roasted over fire) or ensalada malagueña (salad with potatoes, fish, orange, olives, and onion).

In the afternoon, you may travel to Granada, or you can remain in Málaga to view some of the other things that Málaga has to offer, such as:

- The Alameda Principal (Main Avenue) is a boulevard that runs along the Guadalmedina River and features numerous stores, cafés, banks, and hotels. It also has various monuments and structures of importance, such as:

- The Fuente de las Tres Gracias (Fountain of the Three Graces) is a 19th-century fountain with three female figures signifying beauty, charm, and joy.

- The Palacio de la Aduana (Customs Palace) is a 19th-century palace utilized as a customs house and a tobacco factory. It contains the Museum of Malaga, which shows paintings and sculptures from the 15th to 20th century and archaeological objects from numerous eras and civilizations, such as Phoenician, Roman, Visigothic, and Moorish.

- The Parque de Málaga (Málaga Park) is a park that spans the seashore and features several gardens, fountains, sculptures, and seats. It also features various unusual flora and animals from different regions of the globe.

- The Puerto de Málaga (Port of Málaga) is one of Spain's oldest and busiest ports. It has multiple piers, terminals, and warehouses. It also features a promenade, a lighthouse, and a Ferris wheel. It also hosts cruises, ferries, and yachts.

You may conclude your day by eating supper at one of the numerous tapas bars in Málaga, where you can enjoy complimentary tapas with your drink order. You may taste local delicacies, such as berenjenas con miel (fried eggplant with honey) or rabo de toro (bull's tail stew). You may also enjoy live music or flamenco at several places in Málaga, such as La Bulería or El Cardenal.

Day 7: Almuñécar

Almuñécar is a town on the Tropical Coast, a beach resort with a warm temperature and a range of water activities. It is also a town with a long and rich history, including monuments and structures from numerous ages and civilizations. It is also a town that boasts a dynamic and colorful culture, with festivals, markets, and nightlife.

To reach Almuñécar, take a bus or a cab from Granada, which takes around an hour. You may hire a vehicle or join a guided trip to take you there. You should expect to spend at least four hours viewing the major attractions of Almuñécar, but you may certainly spend more time if you want to explore it at your speed.

Almuñécar is a site that will enchant you with its beauty and variety. It is a site that will give you various experiences and activities, from swimming to snorkeling, from sightseeing to shopping. It is a location that will make you feel pleased and comfortable.

Some of the sites that you should not miss in Almuñécar are:

The Castillo de San Miguel (San Miguel fortress) is a fortress that was erected by the Muslims in the 10th century on top of a hill that overlooks the town and the sea. It was utilized as a stronghold and a watchtower until it was seized by Ferdinand II in 1489. It has numerous characteristics, such as:

- The Torre del Homenaje (Tower of Homage) is the castle's tallest tower and gives panoramic views of Almuñécar and the Mediterranean.

- The Patio de Armas (Courtyard of Arms) is the principal courtyard of the castle. It features a cistern, a well, and many barracks.

- The Museo Arqueológico (Archaeological Museum) showcases items from diverse eras and civilizations, such as Phoenician, Roman, Visigothic, Moorish, and Christian.

- The Acueducto Romano (Roman Aqueduct) is an aqueduct constructed by the Romans in the 1st century AD to deliver water to the town. It features many arches and pillars that bridge the valley of the Río Verde (Green River). It is one of the finest surviving Roman aqueducts in Spain.

- The Parque Botánico El Majuelo (Botanical Park El Majuelo) is a park that spans an area of 4 hectares (10 acres) and features more than 200 varieties of plants from various areas of the globe. It also features archaeological remnants from the Phoenician era, such as fish salting facilities and necropolises.

- The Peñón del Santo (Saint's Rock) is a rock that rises above the water and has a crucifix on top. It is also known as Peñón de la Cruz (Rock of the Cross) or Peñón de los Enamorados (Rock of the Lovers). It has various legends linked with it, such as:

- The narrative of Fray Pedro de Zúñiga, who set the cross on the rock in 1509 to celebrate the Christian victory of Almuñécar.

- The tale of Aben Humeya, who hurled himself from the cliff in 1569 after being betrayed by his cousin Aben Aboo during the Morisco insurrection.

- The tale of Isabel de Solís, who leaped from the rock in 1485 after being compelled to marry Boabdil's brother instead of Boabdil himself.

- After seeing Almuñécar, you may eat lunch at one of the neighboring restaurants or cafés, such as La Parra or La Corrala. You may sample some characteristic foods from the shore, such as paella (rice with shellfish) or pescaíto frito (fried fish).

- In the afternoon, you may enjoy some of the beaches and water activities that Almuñécar has to offer, such as:

- The Playa de San Cristóbal (San Cristóbal Beach) is one of the biggest and most popular beaches in Almuñécar. It boasts a great beach, clean water, and a boardwalk with bars, restaurants, and stores. It also features a sculpture of a Phoenician sailor and a tribute to the ocean.

- The Playa de la Herradura (Horseshoe Beach) is one of the most beautiful and natural beaches in

Almuñécar. It boasts gritty sand, turquoise water, and a horseshoe shape. It also boasts a marina, a diving facility, and a castle.

- The Playa de Cantarriján (Cantarriján Beach) is one of the most lonely and wild beaches in Almuñécar. It is in a natural park with stones, clear water, and cliffs. It is also a nudist beach where you may enjoy freedom and the environment.

You may conclude your day by eating supper at one of the numerous tapas bars in Almuñécar, where you can enjoy complimentary tapas with your drink order. You may taste local delicacies, such as espetos de sardinas (sardines skewered on poles and roasted over fire) or pescaíto frito (fried fish). You may also enjoy live music or flamenco at several places in Almuñécar, such as La Cochera or El Chaleco.

CONCLUSION

Granada is a city that will fascinate you with its beauty, its history and its culture. It is a city that will give you a range of experiences, from the magnificent Alhambra to the bustling tapas restaurants, from the icy Sierra Nevada to the warm Mediterranean coast, and from the ancient monuments to the contemporary art. It is a city that will amaze you with its variety and excellence. It is a city that will make you fall in love with it.

On this tour, you have found the finest of Granada, its sights, activities, food and shopping. You have learned about the history and significance of some of Granada's most prominent locations and products, as well as some suggestions and ideas on how to enjoy them. You have also studied the history and culture of Granada, its people, customs and identity.

But this guide is not designed to be comprehensive or final. Granada is a city that has far more to offer than what can be stated in a book. Granada is a city that begs you to explore, discover, and experience. The city awaits you.

How to make the most of your trip: some last suggestions and advice

Granada is a city that will fascinate you with its beauty, charm, and variety. It is a city that offers something for everyone, whether you are interested in history, culture, nature, or nightlife. It is a city that will make you fall in love with its enchantment and mystery. But to get the most out of your vacation, you need to prepare ahead and follow certain suggestions and guidelines. Here are some of them:

When to go: Granada has a Mediterranean climate, with hot and dry summers and warm and rainy winters. The ideal time to visit Granada is in spring or fall when the weather is good and the crowds are lighter. You may also enjoy the festivals and events in these seasons, such as the Holy Week, the International Festival of Music and Dance, or the Jazz Festival. However, if you don't mind the heat or the cold, you can also visit Granada in summer or winter, when you can enjoy the beaches or the ski slopes nearby.

How to get there: Granada has an airport that links with various local and international locations, including Madrid,

Barcelona, London, Paris, and Berlin. You may also take a rail or a bus from other towns in Spain or Europe, such as Seville, Malaga, Cordoba, Valencia, or Lisbon. You may also go to Granada by automobile, but be advised that parking might be difficult and costly in the city center.

How to get around: Granada is a tiny city easily explored on foot, particularly the historical and tourist sites. However, you may also take public transit, such as buses, trams, or taxis, to save time or energy. You may also hire a bike or a scooter to navigate the city in a fun and eco-friendly manner. You may also join a guided tour or a hop-on hop-off bus to view the major sites of Granada.

Where to stay: Granada provides a broad selection of lodging alternatives for various budgets and preferences. You may select hotels, hostels, flats, guesthouses, or cave dwellings. Some of the greatest spots to stay in Granada are:

The Albaicin is the oldest and most picturesque area in Granada, where you can enjoy the breathtaking views of the Alhambra and the city. It is also home to some of the greatest pubs and clubs in Granada, where you can experience the traditional atmosphere of Andalusia. However, be prepared to trek up and down high slopes and steps.

The Realejo: This is the old Jewish district of Granada, where you may discover a blend of history, culture, and modernity. It offers several monuments, museums, and cathedrals to see and stylish boutiques, cafés, and restaurants to enjoy. It is also near to the Alhambra and the city center.

The Zaidín: This is one of Granada's most popular and active areas, where you can discover affordable and colorful hotel alternatives. It offers several bars, pubs, and tapas spots to socialize with residents and students. It is also near the Science Park and the football stadium.

What to see and do: Granada boasts many tourist attractions and activities, ranging from historical sites to natural parks. Some of the must-see sites in Granada are:

The Alhambra: This is the most renowned and stunning sight in Granada, a UNESCO World Heritage Site that shows the beauty of Islamic art and architecture. It is a complex of palaces, gardens, and fortifications erected by the Nasrid sultans during the 13th and 15th centuries. You can enjoy its elaborate decorations, lovely courtyards, imposing towers, and spectacular vistas.

The Generalife: This is the Nasrid Sultans' summer residence and country estate, situated on the slope opposite the Alhambra. It is a masterwork of landscape design, blending aspects of Islamic, Renaissance, and Romantic traditions. It comprises two primary parts: the palace and the gardens. The palace is a small tower that has been changed and rebuilt. It contains two courtyards: the Water Garden Courtyard and the Sultana's Courtyard. The gardens are separated into numerous parts, each with character and beauty.

The Cathedral is one of the most prominent religious structures in Granada, situated in the city's center. It was erected between the 16th and 18th centuries on the site of a medieval mosque. It features a blend of styles, such as Gothic, Renaissance, Baroque, and Neoclassical, but it stands out for its majestic main facade and its enormous dome. It also boasts a magnificent interior, with several chapels, altars, paintings, sculptures, and relics.

The Royal Chapel is the tomb of the Catholic Monarchs Ferdinand and Isabella, who invaded Granada in 1492 and united Spain. It is situated near the Cathedral, and it has a Gothic style. It features a marble mausoleum with the effigies of the kings, as well as their daughter Juana and her husband, Philip. It also features a museum that shows their things, such as their crowns, swords, literature, and costumes.

The Albayzin: This is the historic Moorish district of Granada, situated on the hill opposite the Alhambra. It is a UNESCO World Heritage Site that retains Granada's medieval layout and ambiance. It boasts small lanes, whitewashed buildings, colorful tiles, and secret courtyards. It also has various monuments, like churches, mosques, convents, and palaces. It also boasts various overlooks, such as the Mirador de San Nicolás, where you may enjoy the greatest views of the Alhambra and the city.

The Sacromonte: This is the gypsy neighborhood of Granada, situated on the hill close to the Albayzin. It is famed for its cave dwellings, where many gypsies still reside and do their ancient skills, like pottery or basketry. It is particularly famed for its flamenco concerts, where you can see real singing, dancing, and guitar performances in a cave or a tabla.

The Science Park: This is one of the most visited museums in Spain, situated in the Zaidín area. It is an interactive and informative museum that covers many themes, such as astronomy, biology, physics, chemistry, and ecology. It features numerous pavilions, such as the Planetarium, the Biodome, the Butterfly Garden, and the Observation Tower. It also features temporary exhibits and activities for all ages.

What to eat and drink: Granada has a rich and diverse cuisine that reflects its history and culture. You may discover influences from many cuisines, such as Arabic, Jewish, or Christian. Some of the traditional foods of Granada are:

Tapas: These are small amounts of food served with beverages at taverns and restaurants. Tapas are frequently free in Granada as long as you purchase a drink. However, some venues may charge for or provide various tapas based on the drink you purchase. The best way to enjoy tapas is to travel from bar to bar and taste various sorts of cuisine and beverages. Tapas may be anything from cheese, ham, olives, or bread to meatballs, croquettes, tortillas, or paella.

Gazpacho: This is a cold soup prepared with tomatoes, cucumber, garlic, olive oil, vinegar, and bread. It is pleasant and nourishing, particularly in summer. You may also discover varieties of gazpacho, such as salmorejo (thicker and creamier) or Ajo Blanco (made with almonds and grapes).

Migas: This meal is created of bread crumbs cooked with garlic, olive oil, paprika, and water. It is frequently served with pig products like chorizo, morcilla, or bacon. It is a robust and nourishing meal that originated from the shepherds who used leftover bread to prepare it.

Olla de San Antón: This stew comprises beans, pork ribs, ham bone, potatoes, onion, garlic, bay leaf, and mint. It is customarily eaten on January 17th, the feast day of San Antón (Saint Anthony), the patron saint of animals.

Piononos: These are little pastries of sponge cake drenched in syrup and topped with cream. They are named after Pope Pius IX (Pio Nono in Spanish), who was immensely fond of them. They are characteristic of the town of Santa Fe, near Granada.

Granada also offers a large selection of beverages to match its meals or to refresh oneself. Some of the characteristic beverages of Granada are:

Wine: Granada has various wine districts that create superb wines with varied qualities. Some of the more prominent ones are:

Montefrío: This area produces white wines with fruity flavors and flowery overtones. They are perfect for combining with fish or cheese.

Contraviesa-Alpujarra: This area produces red wines with vivid hues and tastes. They are perfect for combining with meat or cheese.

Alhambra: This area produces red wines with a ruby hue and a pleasant flavor. They are perfect for complementing tapas or desserts.

Beer: Granada has a thriving craft beer sector, with various brewers offering different varieties and beer tastes. You may find them at specialist bars or stores or in some of the tapas establishments that offer them as an alternative to wine. Some of the more prominent ones are:

Cervezas Alhambra is the oldest and most traditional brewery in Granada, established in 1925. It produces different varieties of beer, such as lager, pale ale, bock, or stout. Its main product is the Alhambra Reserva 1925, a premium lager with a golden hue and a rich taste.

Cervezas Nazarí: This is a new and creative brewery in Granada, launched in 2013. It produces beer, such as IPA, wheat, porter, or saison. Its main product is the Nazarí IPA, a hoppy and fruity beer with a bitter aftertaste.

Cervezas La Hermosa: This brewery tap restaurant in Granada where you can enjoy local artisan beers and traditional food. It offers 10 taps with various varieties and tastes of beer, such as blonde, amber, red, or black. You may also purchase bottles or growlers to take away.

Coffee: Granada has had a long and strong coffee culture since the 19th century when the first coffee shops debuted in the city. Today, Granada has several coffee shops serving various coffee varieties, such as espresso, cappuccino, latte, or mocha. You may also discover specialty coffee shops that serve high-quality coffee from various origins and roasts. Some of the top coffee shops in Granada are:

Café Fútbol is one of the most recognizable and historic coffee shops in Granada, situated on Plaza Mariana Pineda. It was created in 1892 and attended by prominent persons such as Federico García Lorca, Manuel de Falla, and Antonio Machado. It is famed for its churros con chocolate (fried dough sticks with hot chocolate), coffee, and sweets.

Café Lisboa is one of the most pleasant and attractive coffee houses in Granada, situated on Calle Reyes Católicos. It boasts a classic aesthetic and courteous service. It serves numerous sorts of coffee, tea, pastries, sandwiches, and salads.

Café 4 Gatos is one of the most contemporary and trendiest coffee shops in Granada, situated on Calle San Jerónimo. It features a simple look and a hipster atmosphere. It provides specialized coffee from diverse sources, roasts, smoothies, juices, and snacks.

Tea: Granada has a significant tea culture inspired by its Arabic background. You may discover several tea stores that provide different tea varieties, such as green, black, white, or herbal. You may also find teterías (tea houses) that sell not only tea but also Arabic sweets, pastries, or hookahs (water pipes). Some of the top tea houses and teterías in Granada are:

La Tetería del Bañuelo is one of the most genuine and traditional tea establishments in Granada, situated on Calle

Bañuelo. It is housed in a 16th-century mansion with a magnificent terrace and a fountain. It serves numerous varieties of tea, such as mint, jasmine, or cinnamon, and Arabic sweets, such as baklava, halva, or kunafa. You may also enjoy live music or poetry readings on various evenings.

La Tetería Alfaguara is one of the most intimate and romantic tea rooms in Granada, situated on Calle Calderería Nueva. It has a Moroccan flair and a friendly environment. It serves numerous sorts of tea, such as rose, orange blossom, or ginger, and pastries, such as muffins, brownies, or cheesecake. You may also enjoy hookahs with various tastes, such as apple, strawberry, or chocolate.

La Tetería Abaco Té: This is one of Granada's most contemporary and attractive tea stores, situated on Calle Puentezuelas. It boasts a simple appearance and a competent service. It sells numerous tea varieties, such as black, green, white, oolong, or rooibos, and accessories, such as teapots, cups, or infusers. You may also purchase tea online or participate in tea tastings or courses.

We have concluded our Granada trip guide 2023-2024. We hope you have read it and found it informative and inspirational for your journey to this great city. Granada is a city that will fascinate you with its beauty, charm, and variety. It is a city that offers something for everyone, whether you are interested in history, culture, nature, or nightlife. It is a city that will make you fall in love with its enchantment and mystery.

Printed in Great Britain
by Amazon

36824804R00136